A
NEW
STU

MW01047242

EARLY LETTERS

HELPS FOR
READING AND UNDERSTANDING
THE MESSAGE

Bob Young

James Kay Publishing

Tulsa, Oklahoma

A Series of New Testament Study Guides
EARLY LETTERS
Helps for Reading and Understanding the Message
ISBN 978-1-943245-52-9
Second Edition

www.bobyoungresources.com

www.jameskaypublishing.com
e-mail: sales@jameskaypublishing.com

© 2017 Bob Young
Cover design by Bob & Jan Young
Author Photo by Jan Young

Table of Contents

Preface to the Series

A number of factors have converged in my life as influences on my method of Bible study and Bible teaching. My undergraduate training in Bible and biblical languages served as the foundation for 25 years of full-time preaching ministry. During those years in ministry, I periodically took graduate coursework in an effort to stay fresh.

When I decided to pursue graduate education diligently, I already loved teaching from an exegetical viewpoint while paying special attention to the historical-cultural context and the grammatical-syntactical features of the biblical text. I had seen the healthy ways in which people respond to thoughtful efforts to explain and apply the message of the Bible. I had developed the habit of using that same kind of Bible study in my sermon preparation. For those reasons, I focused my graduate training in ministry dynamics and how to integrate academic studies with practical applications. Because I did graduate work while continuing full-time work in ministry, I was blessed to have a laboratory to apply and test what I was learning.

My years of teaching and administration in Christian higher education coupled with increased involvement in the world of missions have made me even more aware of the need to view the Bible, insofar as possible, outside one's own social, cultural, experiential, and religious backgrounds. My interpretative efforts today are influenced by my training and experience. I try to understand the biblical context, the historical-cultural context, and the literary context—vocabulary, genres, grammar, and syntax. I try to understand the original message of the author and the purpose of the text as first steps toward understanding the message of the text in today's world. I want to know what the text said and what it meant, so that I can know what it says and what it means today.

As I have prepared these study guides, I have constantly asked myself, "What would I want in a study guide to the biblical text?" I have been guided by this question, at times excluding technical details and academic questions, at other times including such items because of their value in understanding and communicating the text. Above all, I have tried to provide a practical study guide to put in clear relief what the text says as a first step toward valid interpretation of what the text means and how it should be applied today.

I wrote these guides with multiple readers in mind. There is little new in these volumes, but preachers and Bible class teachers will be helped with their study and review of the text. Christians who have an interest in the message of the Bible will be helped by the textual jewels and the summaries that are included. The initial motivation to prepare these volumes came from my desire to provide a resource that will be translated into Spanish, keeping in mind the needs of preachers, Bible teachers, and Christians who do not have access to the many resources and books that exist in English. A good way to describe these guides is that they are simple explanations designed to help with the task of understanding and applying the biblical text. A few technical details are included to help with understanding, to identify repeated words or themes, and to give insights into the message of the text. May God bless you in your desire and your efforts to understand and apply the message of the Bible!

Introduction to the Series

The Purpose of These Guides

To describe the publications included in this series as "Bible study guides" says something about their intended purpose. As guides, these little books do not attempt to answer every question that may arise in your study of the biblical text. They are not commentaries in the strictest sense of the word. The focus of these guides is distinct.

I have as a primary goal to encourage you to do your own study of the Bible. This series of study guides is designed to assist the Bible student with preliminary and basic exegetical work, and to suggest some study methods that will enrich your study and help you identify the message of the text—whether in a specific verse or paragraph, a larger context, or an entire book of the New Testament. A primary goal of these guides is to help you maintain a focus on the purpose and message of the original author. The message of the original writer should inform our understanding of the text and its application today. One should not think that the message and meaning of the text today would be significantly different than the message and meaning of the original document.

The title also says that these guides are "helps." I have tried to provide resources to guide and enrich your study, keeping the purpose of the original author in view. This desire has informed the content of these study guides. Many study guides exist and there is no need to write more books that basically have the same content. Generally, the information included in these guides is designed to help identify the purpose of the original author and the message of the Bible. In some passages, the information included in these guides will provide insights not readily available in other resources.

What Kinds of "Helps" Are Included in These Guides?

These study guides reflect how I organize and understand the text of the Bible, taking into account various exegetical factors such as syntax, grammar, and vocabulary. Along the way, I share some observations that will help clarify passages that are difficult to understand. I have not tried to comment on every passage where potential problems or differences in understanding exist. I have not noted every textual variant in the original text. At times these notes may seem to be unnecessary comments on passages where the meaning is clear; that probably means I am trying to share insights to deepen understanding and appreciation of the text. In other passages, some may ask why I have not included more comments or explanation. Such is the individualized nature of Bible study. The overall goal of my comments is to help maintain a focus on the original author's message and purpose for writing—the "what it said and what it meant" of the original author in the original context.

For each chapter, there is a "Content" section that usually includes a brief outline, followed by notes ("Study Helps") about the biblical text. The content sections of these guides, including how the text is divided and how paragraphs are described, are drawn from my own reading and analysis of the text and from a comparison of several translations. In only a very few cases does the outline provided in this guide vary from the majority opinion, and those cases are noted and the reasons given. In some chapters, there is an overview with introductory comments to help orient the student to the overall content and message of the chapter. In a few chapters, there are some additional observations. Often, a paraphrased summary is included as part of the textual notes or in a separate section after the study helps. As noted above, the comments are not intended to answer every question. In a few cases, I have addressed topics that are not treated in detail in other resources. Texts that are easily understood and matters that are customarily included in other resources are, for the most part, not treated in detail here.

A Useful Tool for Understanding the Message of the Bible

While the primary purpose of these guides is to assist in personal study of the biblical text, these guides will also serve the casual reader who wants to understand the basic message of the Bible. The guides are written in such a way that the reader can understand the general message of the text, along with some interesting and helpful details, simply by reading the guide. One might describe theses guides as a kind of "CliffsNotes" to the Bible, but they are intended as helps and should not be thought of as taking the place of Bible reading and Bible study.

How to Use This Bible Study Guide in Personal Bible Study

This guide is not intended to take the place of your own Bible reading and study but is intended to provide insights and suggestions as you read the Bible, and to be a resource that will help you check your understanding. **You are encouraged to use this guide and your own Bible side by side.** Some sections of this guide may be difficult to understand unless one can identify the specific part of the text that is being described or explained.

No specific translation of the biblical text is included in this guide. Two goals influenced the decision not to include a translation of the biblical text. First, it is hoped that you will be encouraged to use your own study Bible. Second, these notes are designed to be helpful in biblical study regardless of the version the reader may prefer for personal Bible study.

My primary purpose is to make it easier for you, the reader and student, to analyze and understand the text. Ultimately, you are responsible for your own interpretation of the Bible and you cannot simply follow what a favorite preacher or commentator says. Often the study notes for a chapter or subsection of a chapter are followed by a brief summary of the content, focusing on the message.

Five Steps for Bible Study. The suggested process for effectively using these Bible study guides involves five steps. First, you should read an introduction to the book of the Bible you wish to study. The introductions provided in these guides will serve well. They are for the most part briefer than normal and do not cover every detail. In this series of guides, sometimes one introduction is provided to cover multiple books, as in the case of the Thessalonian correspondence and the Pastoral Letters.

The second step in your study is to read through the book of the Bible you wish to study to understand the overall content. It will be helpful if this can be done at a single sitting. The student facing time constraints may have time for only one reading, but multiple readings will reveal additional details of the book, providing you an opportunity to notice repeated words and phrases and to think about the message of the book, how the book develops its message, and how various parts of the book are connected. You will find help for your reading in the chapter outlines that are provided in these study guides.

Now you are ready to begin your study of individual chapters or sections. The process is simple: read a section of the text until you have a good understanding of it. This is not an in-depth reading to resolve every question but is a general reading to understand the content of the passage.

The fourth step is for you to write your own outline of the chapter or section, with paragraphing that reflects major thought patterns, divisions, and topics. In these study guides, each chapter has a section with suggested paragraphing based on a comparison of various translations. While it is possible to skip this step in which you do your own analysis and paragraphing, and to move directly to the paragraphing provided in the study guide, this is not the recommended approach. You will benefit from taking the time and investing the energy to do this work in initial reading and understanding.

Finally, the study guides have a section of study helps that will help you read and understand the text and keep the intent of the original author in mind as you do more focused study. In many chapters, a final section that summarizes the message of the chapter is included.

Initial Reading and Paragraphing

In other articles and publications, I have explained the importance of preparatory reading and personal study of the biblical text. In the five-step process described above, initial reading and paragraphing occur in the second, third, and fourth steps. When the student carefully works through these steps, it becomes clear that this is a "Bible" study and is not simply a process of reading more background information and commentary from a human author who is trying to explain the Bible. Although many students jump immediately from reading an introduction to reading a commentary, it is important that the student learn to read and study the Bible for herself or himself. Once the biblical text is familiar, I suggest the student think about the themes that can be identified and how to mark the paragraph divisions, based on the content of the passage and the subjects treated. Once this work is complete, it is good to compare the resulting paragraphing with that of several versions, or with the outlines in the content sections of these guides.

A Note About Paragraphing

Paragraph divisions are the key to understanding and following the original author's message. Most modern translations are divided into paragraphs and provide a summary heading. Ideally, every paragraph has one central topic, truth, or thought. Often, there will be several ways to describe the subject of the paragraph. Only when we understand the original author's message by following his logic and presentation can we truly understand the Bible. Only the original author is inspired—readers must take care not to change or modify the message. A first step toward integrity with the text is to develop the ability to analyze it and establish paragraphs.

Note: This introductory information is not repeated in each chapter of this guide. Readers will find it helpful to return to this introductory section again and again to guide their study, especially before beginning the study of a new chapter of the Bible.

A Word About Formatting

The format of the Study Helps in each chapter follows the outline that is provided for the chapter. The major points of the outline are used to begin new sections of the Study Helps. Biblical references that introduce sections or subsections of the Study Helps are placed in bold type to assist the student. In the case of paragraphs that cover multiple verses, the biblical references are placed in progressive order on the basis of the first verse in the citation.

Standard abbreviations of biblical books are used. Verse citations that do not include the name of a book (e.g. 2:14) refer to the book being studied. Abbreviations that may not be familiar to some readers include the following: cf. = compare; e.g. = for example; v. = verse; vv. = verses.

The first time a translation is mentioned, the standard abbreviation is included for translations that are less well-known. Subsequent references use only the abbreviation.

Greek words are placed in italics. Often, the corresponding Greek word, a literal meaning, and other translation possibilities are placed in parentheses immediately after an English word. Greek words are written as transliterations in English letters, using the basic lexical form of the word. It is hoped that this will make it easier for the reader without a knowledge of Greek. Many readers will find these references interesting, especially in those passages where there is repeated use of the same Greek word. Readers can quickly pass over this inserted parenthetical information if desired.

In a few cases, parentheses are used to indicate Greek verbal forms or noun forms where this information would be significant to the student with some understanding of grammar. The Greek language uses three classes of conditional statements: clauses that begin with "if." These constructions are noted when the use is significant. The first class condition is assumed to be true from the viewpoint of the author. The second class condition is contrary to fact. The third class condition is hypothetical. Again, the reader can pass over this information rapidly if desired.

The Greek text used is the 27th edition of *Novum Testamentus Graece* which is identical with the 4th revised edition of *The Greek New Testament*.

Quotation marks are often used to call attention to special words or topics, and also to indicate citations or translations of the biblical text, most of which are my own. This is done to help the reader identify references to the biblical text, since no specific translation of the biblical text is included in this Study Guide.

Parentheses are used liberally to enclose information and comments that would often be included in footnotes. It is hoped that readers will find this more convenient, both those who want to read the expanded explanation and those who wish to skip over the parenthetical material.

Comments concerning contemporary applications of the text are limited, but are included from time to time.

Summaries are provided for many chapters, with the goal of helping to make the message of the chapter clearer. Some of these summaries are paraphrases, some are written in first person, from the standpoint of the author; others are written in third person and are explanations of the content. Summaries written in either the first person or third person are not translations and they are not paraphrasing. They are attempts to communicate the basic points and the purpose of the original message.

Introduction to Galatians

Background

Galatians is one of the earliest writings of the New Testament. It has been called "the Magna Carta of Christian liberty." Written to combat the influence of Judaizing teachers in the Galatian churches, its primary message is that nothing is needed for salvation but Christ. This letter, along with the book of Romans, was an important factor in the beginning of the Protestant Reformation. Luther said, "The little book of Galatians is my letter; I have betrothed myself to it; it is my wife."

Galatians is part autobiography, part doctrine, and part practical instruction. It counteracts the influence of the Judaizing teachers by showing that salvation in Christ is available apart from Judaism's emphasis on righteousness by works. The conflict between Christianity and Judaism often focused on circumcision. Especially during the first two decades after the establishment of the church, many Jewish Christians believed that Gentiles should be circumcised to be Christians. The book of Galatians makes clear that requiring Gentiles to participate in circumcision in order to become Christians denies the efficacy of the sacrifice of Jesus.

From another perspective, the book of Galatians can be described as Paul's missionary manual, showing how he worked to resolve a major problem that had arisen in some recently established churches. Paul was writing to churches he himself had established. (An explanation of the two major views concerning the destination of the letter is included below in the discussion about the recipients of the letter.)

Galatians is about "getting the gospel message right" and "getting the right gospel message." When the gospel message is changed, the impact of the gospel in the lives of the hearers is also changed. I often summarize Paul's message in Galatians like this: the "too hard" gospel adds human requirements so that it is impossibly difficult; the "too soft" gospel does not result in true liberty since it cannot advance love and cannot avoid license; the "just right" gospel encourages a life lived through

Christ's presence, understands that everyone is an heir in Christ, and is fulfilled by walking in the Spirit. In Galatians Paul compares these different "gospels," pointing to the fact that in reality there is only one gospel. His purpose is to show that the gospel he has proclaimed is the only gospel by which God justifies believers and empowers changed lives.

The message of Galatians is still needed today, especially in view of the fact that in Christianity one still finds some preaching a "too hard" gospel and others preaching a "too soft" gospel. Some still add humanly devised requirements to the gospel, some soften or eliminate the biblical faith response to the gospel, and others accept persons based on verbal profession regardless of lifestyle. Galatians makes clear three things: that a person is not required to "prove" faith through certain actions before obeying the gospel, that accepting the gospel by obedient faith does not make salvation meritorious, and that those who accept the gospel are called to walk by the Spirit and not according to the world.

In summary, Paul addresses two extremes in the book of Galatians. On the one hand one must not add requirements to the gospel of Jesus; on the other hand, genuine Christian liberty does not lead to license. The gospel does not lead to legalism; the gospel does not lead to license. The contrast between these two "false gospels" is further explained in the "Study Helps" sections below.

Authorship, Recipients, and Date

Author. Paul is identified as the author. The autobiographical section of the letter supports the identification.

Recipients and Date. The date assigned to the letter depends on the identity of the recipients. The two theories concerning the recipients of the letter are typically called the "Northern Galatian Theory" and the "Southern Galatian Theory." The first sees Galatia as composed of the ethnic Galatians of north central Turkey (Asia Minor). There is no biblical evidence that Paul visited this region, although such a visit would have been possible early on the second journey. The book of Galatians is usually assigned a date in the mid-50s with this theory. The second theory, the "Southern Galatian Theory," identifies the Galatian churches as those established on the first missionary journey in the southern cities of Antioch of Pisidia, Lystra, Derbe, and Iconium. In this view, Galatia is not an ethnic region but an administrative area. If Paul is writing to the churches he has recently established, an earlier date is assigned to the book. The subject of Galatians aligns with and closely corresponds to the subject of the Jerusalem meeting in Acts 15 (AD 50). Paul could have written Galatians before the Acts 15 meeting, but it is more likely that he wrote after receiving a consensus opinion from the church leaders and the church in Jerusalem (thus assigning a date of AD 50-51 to the book). This date makes Galatians the first Pauline letter in the New Testament. The later date ("Northern Galatian Theory") places the book in the same approximate time frame as the Thessalonian letters or perhaps a little later (AD 52-53). Galatians is placed first in this Bible Study Guide because of the order of the books in our Bibles.

PROBABLE TIMELINE OF PAUL'S EARLY LIFE

AD 30	Ac 2	Pentecost
AD 31	Ac 7-8	Paul was present at death of Stephen
AD 32-33	Ac 9	Paul becomes a Christian
AD 33-36	Gal 1	In Arabia, went to Jerusalem 3 years later
AD 36-47	Ac 9, 11, 12	Cilicia, Antioch, Jerusalem visit with funds for the poor
AD 48-49	Ac 13-14	First missionary Journey
AD 49-50	Ac 15, Gal 2	Jerusalem meeting

Note: See additional information in comments on Galatians 2.

Several other factors are often cited in establishing a date for the book. Galatians does not mention Silas or Timothy but mentions Barnabas three times, which better fits the first journey. The visit to Jerusalem (Gal. 2:1-10) could be a visit not mentioned in Acts or it could be the visit to participate in the Jerusalem meeting. Some think the interaction with Peter (Gal. 2:11-14) concerning fellowship with the Gentiles suggests a date for Galatians before the Jerusalem meeting. In this Bible study guide, Galatians is analyzed from the viewpoint that Paul is writing to the churches he had recently worked to establish, probably very shortly after the Jerusalem meeting of Acts 15.

To justify narrowing the time frame for Galatians to the years immediately before or immediately after the Jerusalem conference, one must analyze what the Bible says about Paul's activities and his visits to Jerusalem. Acts records three visits of Paul to Jerusalem: Acts 9:26-30, after his conversion; Acts 11:30, 12:25, to deliver famine relief funds; and Acts 15:1-30, the Jerusalem meeting. Galatians records two visits: Gal. 1:18, after three years; and Gal. 2:1, after fourteen years. The references in Galatians suggest that as much as 17 years passed after Paul's conversion before the visit mentioned in Gal. 2:1. (It is possible that the 14 years of Gal. 2:1 includes the 3 years of Gal. 1:18, but since both references occur in the same context, it is more likely that they should be considered consecutively as a 17-year time span.) The question of chronology must reconcile the accounts of Acts and Galatians, recognizing that the different details can be explained by different perspectives, different authors, and the different purposes of Luke and Paul in the books they authored.

What is learned by the reconstruction of the timeline of Paul's life? (See "Probable Timeline" chart above.) If Paul was converted (Acts 9) within a short period of time after Pentecost, his conversion could be as early as AD 31-33. (In this study, the time frames are reconstructed on the basis of dating Pentecost in AD 30.) That would place the Gal. 1:18 visit in AD 34-36 (and present the possibility that the Gal. 1:18 visit could be reconciled with the Acts 9:26 visit). Paul then went to Cilicia (Acts 9, 11-12; Gal. 1), and later spent a year in Antioch (Acts 11:25-26). He made a visit to Jerusalem in Acts 11-12. He made the first missionary journey in AD 48-49. The most difficult challenge in establishing an early timeline is that it is difficult to fit in the seventeen years of Gal. 1 and Gal. 2 between Paul's conversion and the first journey. Such would require Paul's conversion in AD 30 or 31, almost immediately after Pentecost. The most likely option is that the Jerusalem visit of Gal. 2:1 (after 14 years) is the same visit as Acts 15. Perhaps the meeting described in Galatians 2 occurred before the more official meeting recorded in Acts 15. The timeline used in this study places the writing of Galatians shortly after the Jerusalem assembly of Acts 15.

Here is a timeline for Paul's letters, including approximate dates (AD), locations, and relationship to the book of Acts. The date of Paul's first visit to Corinth can be established without question based on the reference to Gallio in Acts 18.

Date	Location	Bible Text	Letters Written by Paul
50	Jerusalem assembly	Acts 15	Gal written around this date
51-52	Paul in Corinth 18 months	Acts 18	1-2 Thess written around this date
53-56	Paul in Ephesus 3 years	Acts 19	1-2 Cor, Rom written during this time
	Overland trip	Acts 19-20	
58-60	In Jerusalem and Caesarea	Acts 21-26	("a little over 2 years")
60-62	First Roman Imprisonment	Acts 27-28	wrote Eph, Phil, Col, Philm
63-66	Additional travels	after Acts	wrote 1 Timothy, Titus
66-68	Last imprisonment	after Acts	wrote 2 Timothy

Purpose of the Letter

By surveying the content of the letter, we can say that Paul wanted to accomplish at least the following: (1) defend the authority and independence of his apostleship; (2) demonstrate the authority of his gospel based on God's purpose, his independence, and his acceptance by the apostles; (3) resolve the problem of the "too hard" gospel in which Gentiles were being required to fulfill various requirements of Judaism in order to be faithful Christians; (4) make certain that Christian liberty did not degenerate into "too soft" license and excess; (5) explain that the gospel does not depend on law but rather on the promise that came before the law, and (6) support the truth that the gospel delivers one to a life lived in the Spirit.

Overview of the Letter

1-2 --Prologue, warning against any other gospel than the one preached by Paul and received by the Galatians (1:1-10)
--Autobiographical section to explain and defend Paul's apostleship
--Paul's call by God
--Paul's interaction with other apostles was one of independence; his interaction with Jewish leaders in Jerusalem shows that he was recognized by them; his

interaction with Peter shows acceptance of the gospel Paul preached

--Paul's manner of life had been totally changed

3-4   --Contrast of the law and the Spirit

--Contrast of the law and the promise

--Sons of God by faith in Christ

--Paul appeals to his personal relationship with the Galatians

--Paul explains the relationship between Judaism and Christian faith through an allegory based on the Old Testament story of Hagar and Sarah

5-6   --Freedom in Christ is based on love and avoids indulgence

--Life in Christ is by the Spirit

--Caring and relating through a new vantage point: not circumcision but the cross

--Closing remarks

Some outline the book by using the typical sequence of doctrinal and practical sections (1-4, 5-6). I think it better to see three sections: autobiographical and defense of apostleship (1-2), doctrinal (3-4), and practical (5-6).

A Few Other Matters

In this volume, a summary of the message of Galatians appears in a separate section—immediately after this introduction. (In the treatment of the Thessalonian correspondence, a summary of the message of the chapter is included with the outline, overview and observations at the beginning of each chapter.)

No footnotes are included in these Bible Study Guides; the content is general knowledge. No bibliography is supplied; I have worked primarily from the biblical text and from my own notes. As I began working on this project, thinking about various design and formatting elements, and preparing these written notes, I was impressed by the work of Bob Utley. That influence is apparent at times in my explanations and a few sections of these notes reflect his treatment of the text.

Summary of the Message of Galatians

Chapter 1

Greetings, from Paul, an apostle by God's will! Jesus' death and resurrection rescued us from this sinful world in which we live. We need to talk about that gospel.

The gospel I preached to you is the only gospel; there is no other gospel even remotely like it. No one has a right to change it—not even angels or preachers who claim special insights. I am surprised you are so quickly turning away to a totally different gospel message.

I received my apostleship and my gospel independently. I am trying only to please God; I am not concerned with whether other people are pleased.

I was called by God to be an apostle and to proclaim the gospel to Gentiles. My gospel came from Jesus, and I am fulfilling God's purpose for me as I preach to the Gentiles.

I visited Jerusalem three years after I became a follower of Christ, but I did not have much contact with the other apostles. I certainly did not go up to Jerusalem to get my gospel message "straight" or to make certain that others liked what I was doing in preaching to the Gentiles. Thankfully, the churches praised God because of me!

Chapter 2

When I again went up to Jerusalem 14 years later, my apostleship and my work in preaching the gospel to the Gentiles were recognized. Yes, there were some who tried to cast doubt on our Christian freedom. They were concerned that such a gospel message had no relationship to the Jewish law. The main leaders in Jerusalem, however, extended full fellowship to me; and they agreed that Titus, being a Gentile, did not have to be circumcised to be a Christian.

I remind you also that one time in Antioch, when Peter was being inconsistent in his attitude and acceptance of the Gentiles because Jewish visitors had come from Jerusalem, I rebuked him publicly because many others were following his bad example.

You can evaluate what I am preaching for yourselves. The gospel says that justification in Christ is through faith and does not depend on the law. The law only defined sin and pointed to the need for forgiveness. God used the law for that purpose, but that does not make God a servant of the law to advance the law. Jesus' death was necessary because of sin, and sin was made known through the law, but that does not mean that Jesus was advancing either sin or the law. Actually, the message of the law is that the law should be left behind in favor of God's grace in Christ. God used the law to usher in grace; the law exalts grace.

Through the law I died to the law so I could live for God. I died by being crucified with Christ so Christ could live in me. Justification could never come through the law. The death of Christ was the only answer, and the gospel I am preaching is the gospel of God's grace—the same thing the law was saying!

Chapter 3

How foolish can you be? Is this really that hard? Think about it. Law or faith? The answer is obvious.

Abraham is an example of how faith was active without any relationship to the law—four centuries before the law was given. The promise came first and never depended on the law. The promise saw in advance that God would justify the Gentiles by faith. Further, the promise to Abraham can never be changed because it was confirmed by God himself.

The law itself speaks of the curse that it brings to those who try to live by it. Justification on the basis of the law is impossible because no one can keep the law. The law results in curses, not blessings.

Consider the law and the promise—which came first? What was God's purpose in the promise? God purposed to bless all nations through Abraham's seed—singular, specifically referring to the coming of Christ and the gospel. What was God's purpose in the law? The law was temporary, lasting until Christ should come, pointing to faith in Christ. Once the goal of the law was reached, the law was no longer needed.

Inheritance cannot be both by law and by promise. Inheritance comes through the promise by faith. This is what the law was pointing to. We are all sons of Abraham (and thus included in the promise) through faith in Christ. This becomes clear when you understand that baptism is the process of being clothed with Christ.

All of the distinctions that excluded people under the law—ethnicity, social and economic status, gender—are now removed so that everyone can be a "son of God" with access to the inheritance. Everyone who is "in Christ" is of the seed of Abraham and is an heir according to the promise, not on the basis of the law.

Chapter 4

I want to say a little more about how important this is. Because all of you are sons by faith in Christ, all of you are heirs. When the son is a child, one can hardly tell the difference between the son who is an heir and a slave child of the same age. Neither has any control over details of his life. The law made us slaves; Jesus makes us sons. God acted at just the right time. We know we are sons because God has given us his Spirit so we can have an intimate relationship with him as our Father.

I am afraid for you. Please consider what I am saying. To reject the pure gospel is to reject the privilege of being a son and to return to slavery. When I first came to you, you accepted the gospel and you also accepted me, despite my physical condition. What has changed? I sincerely sought your well-being so that you were included in Christ. Now you are listening to false teachers who are trying to exclude you. Zeal is a good quality, but it is better when it unselfishly seeks what is best. I am still concerned for your well-being—I want Christ to be formed in you.

An allegory will illustrate the contrast. The story of Hagar and Sarah shows that God's purpose has always focused on freedom rather than bondage. In this story, we can see the contrast between the promise and the law; we can see two covenants, the first depending on the law and the second depending on the promise that was fulfilled in Christ.

Chapter 5

Here is what this means. Christ came to bring you freedom. You will never know that freedom by going back to the slavery of the law. Here is something impossible—that circumcision and Christ both have value at the same time! Here is another impossibility—when circumcision is given value, one is obligated to observe the whole law—something that is impossible. Even though the law was pointing to grace, there is no room for grace while the law is in effect. Faith in Christ brings hope, righteousness, and the Spirit. Christ brings a new life of faith and love.

Surely you would not go back! Freedom in Christ is the only power that will let us escape the sinful desires the law arouses. If you doubt that focusing on the law leads to bad behavior, look at the teachers who are biting and destroying one another and everything around them. That is the result of their "gospel which is no gospel."

The new life in Christ is possible because of the Spirit's guiding presence as we live in the Spirit. That is the only way to get rid of the old life once and for all. The old worldly life and the new spiritual life are opposites. The Christian life is "Spirit controlled," and there is no need for any other guidance system (like the law!). The Spirit produces an entirely different kind of life in comparison to the evil desires that are constantly aroused by a "law system" that depends on keeping a list of prohibitions in mind. Those in Christ crucify the flesh and live according to the Spirit.

Chapter 6

Here is what life in the Spirit looks like. We help one another avoid sin, we carefully restore those who fall, we avoid temptations, we carry burdens, we love our neighbors, we avoid conceit, we take care of our own responsibilities. God understands everything and takes everything into account. He is never deceived. Whether we live by the flesh or by the Spirit, we will reap accordingly. Keep on doing good, especially to one another.

Here is the conclusion: the Christian life is not measured by circumcision, obedience to the law, and boasting about such things. The only boasting in Christ is in the cross. The cross represents Jesus' crucifixion, but it also represents my crucifixion to the world. What counts in Christ is being a new creation, following peace, and understanding mercy.

I pray that the way can be opened for preaching the gospel to the Gentiles and that future troubles can be avoided. Grace be yours!

Galatians 1

[Note: it is suggested that the student read the introductory materials in this guide before beginning any individual preparatory reading and analysis. The greatest benefit will be gained by following carefully the five steps outlined in the introduction.]

CONTENT

The paragraphing included in the Content section of each chapter is only a suggestion. The student is encouraged to identify the paragraphs and subsections within each paragraph to assist in personal study. In this chapter, the division of the biblical text into paragraphs is fairly standard in modern translations (see comment below about v. 10).

Outline of the Chapter
1:1-5	Greeting or salutation
1:6-10	There is only one gospel, there is no other gospel like it*
1:11-17	Paul's apostleship, called by God
1:18-24	Paul's visit to Jerusalem after three years

There is a question about the paragraph division. For example, NET divides 6-9 and 10-17. See additional explanation below in the Study Helps.

Overview of the Chapter

1:1-5, this is one sentence in Greek

1:6-10, in the book of Galatians, the normal thanksgiving and prayer are absent, perhaps reflecting the tension between Paul and his readers; Paul goes directly to the theme or purpose of the book—a warning against a "new gospel" that had been introduced

1:11-17, these verses introduce an extended autobiographical section that extends through Chapter 2; Paul's purpose is to defend his apostleship and the gospel he is proclaiming to the Gentiles

1:18-24, Paul's time in isolation, his visit to Jerusalem after three years, and his lack of contact with the other apostles show his independence

<u>Summary of the Chapter</u>
        The salutation of the book includes the typical items of author, greetings, and recipients, but the prayer and thanksgiving are absent. Instead Paul includes a summary of the gospel, a bridge that moves immediately to his purpose for writing: to address the problem of abandoning the genuine gospel. No one has the right to change the gospel, not even an angel, and certainly no preacher, including Paul and his fellow-evangelists.
        Those who are trying to please God will not keep their eyes on what pleases other people. In this contrast, Paul addresses an important problem that comes with the alternate version of the gospel. Paul's own experience with the gospel was independent of human influences. He received the gospel directly from Jesus Christ, and he was not seeking to please other people when he received it; in fact, the gospel in his life had led him in totally new directions. After receiving the gospel, his priority was simply to please God. He did not try to verify that the gospel he received would be accepted by others; in fact, for quite some time he was isolated from other Christians. Eventually, he did go up to Jerusalem and was able to make Peter's acquaintance; but he did not go to Jerusalem in order to get his gospel "straight," and his contact with other Christian leaders was very limited.
        This history demonstrates that the gospel he had preached in the Galatian churches was authentic, especially his presentation of the gospel to the Gentiles. Preaching to the Gentiles was the task to which God had called him. That the gospel Paul preached was authentic was also the verdict of the churches in Judea, even though they did not know him and were only hearing about his preaching. The gospel Paul had preached to the Gentiles was from Jesus, was according to God's purpose in Paul's life, and had been praised by Christian leaders and the Christian communities in Jerusalem and Judea.

Paul's point is that the gospel he originally preached in Galatia should not be changed by adding new requirements. He will reinforce this point throughout the book.

STUDY HELPS
1:1-5. These verses are one long sentence in Greek. Paul is identified as the author, asserting even in the greeting his divine authority as God's representative, anticipating that the letter will serve to refute any contrary claims. He identifies himself as an apostle in the best sense of the word—one sent by Jesus Christ and God the Father. This also means that he has received the content of his gospel through divine revelation. Paul was not an apostle according to the criteria of Acts 1, but was an apostle "called out of due season." (For more on the use of the word apostle in the New Testament, see the comments at 1:18-19.) The brothers who are with Paul are not named. The letter is unique in that it was sent to a group of churches in a specific region and is named for the region; however, some also see Ephesians as a letter intended for a group of churches.

1:3. Grace and peace are common elements in Paul's use of the Greek epistolary form.

1:4-5. Paul introduces the major points of his gospel: (1) the resurrection of Jesus by God's power; (2) Christ's substitutionary death; (3) rescue and escape from the present age; (4) according to God's eternal will. Jesus gave himself to deliver us (*exaireo*, rescue, pluck out, thus to set free or to liberate). The last two translation possibilities reflect a theme of the letter; see Chapters 5-6 for the development of the theme of freedom. That "Jesus gave himself to deliver us" shows the shared purpose and unity of the Godhead. We must not read Scripture trying to manufacture conflicts. The question of who gave Jesus as a sacrifice is not presented as an "either-or" option. God gave his Son. Jesus gave himself. Both are true.

We are rescued from this present evil age (*aion*, time period, world, extended situation).

1:5. "To whom be glory" serves as a brief word of praise (laudation), a part of the typical Greek letter form.

1:6-9 (10). Paul says that the Galatians are turning away from the gospel because of the influence of those who are teaching another gospel. "So quickly" may refer to (1) the fact that only a brief time has passed since they accepted the gospel Paul preached, (2) a brief time after Paul's departure, or (3) how quickly they had changed their thinking once the false teaching was presented. All three possibilities make sense in the context of Galatians. The word Paul uses for turning away (*metatithemi*, transfer, replace, exchange) is often translated "deserting." Used in this sense, it was a military term. The Galatians turned away by rejecting Paul's gospel. They were accepting a substitute gospel as a replacement or exchange; they were changing sides. They were not only rejecting Paul, they were rejecting God who called them by grace.

They were following a different (*heteros,* different, not only different but "entirely different") gospel. Paul continues by saying that the different gospel they are following is not a gospel that is "a little different but is still similar" (*allos*, meaning different, but "of the same kind"). The two words that are translated as "different" were sometimes synonyms with little distinction in the first century, but in this passage, it seems that Paul wants to make the distinction: the gospel the Galatians were turning to was "totally different," not just "a little different but still of the same basic kind." Various translations make the distinction in different ways. The NRSV says, "…not that there is another gospel." There are not two gospels. There are not two almost alike versions of the same gospel. What the Galatians were following was so different that it did not qualify to be called gospel. It was a perverted version of the gospel.

"…so soon you are deserting to an entirely different gospel, which is not in any way like the gospel, because some are disturbing you and wanting to distort the gospel of Christ."
Gal. 1:6-7

Some were troubling them and distorting (*metastrepho*, to corrupt) the gospel. The distortion centered in the necessity of following Jewish customs, traditions, and teachings in order to be accepted as a Christian.

1:8. "Even if" is hypothetical (third class condition). It is unlikely that an angel or any companion of Paul would preach such a gospel. Regardless, anyone who preaches a gospel contrary to the gospel preached by Paul and his companions is anathema (accursed, cut off). The almost parallel construction in 1:9 is assumed to be true (first class condition). The false teaching is not just hypothetical. It is in fact occurring. This construction serves to accentuate Paul's point: such teachers and teaching are to be rejected!

1:9. This verse (with a construction that parallels v. 8) serves well to summarize the entire paragraph (vv. 6-9) and to accentuate Paul's purpose for writing. These verses are the theme verses of the book.

1:10. There is a question concerning paragraphing. Does this verse belong with vv. 6-9, or is it the beginning of a new section? It is easy to understand this verse as the beginning of the autobiographical section, but some identify the autobiographical section as beginning in v. 11. Paul makes clear that he is seeking to please God, not human beings. In contrast, in v. 14 he describes a time in his life when he was trying to please human beings. This verse (1:10) provides closure to the first ten verses and provides a transition to the following section where Paul shows that he was not in any way dependent on what human beings were teaching, saying, or thinking. The "if" of v. 10 is "contrary to fact" (second class condition). The meaning is made clear by translating with a parenthetical insertion: "If I were still trying to please men (which I am not) ...." Paul is first and foremost a slave of Jesus because Jesus is his Lord. The question concerning paragraphing is reflected in this guide by separating the comments for this verse from both the previous section and the following section.

1:11-17. These verses are the first paragraph in an extended literary unit (1:11-2:14). In an extended autobiographical summary, Paul mentions various aspects of his apostleship to demonstrate the validity of the gospel message he proclaims.

Here is a brief overview of the development of Paul's defense: Paul was called by God and received his message directly (1:11-17); he did not consult with other apostles when he went to Jerusalem after 3 years (1:18-24); he was accepted by the "pillars" in Jerusalem on a subsequent visit after 14 years (2:1-10); he successfully opposed Peter in defense of his gospel to the Gentiles (2:11-14).

1:11-12. The gospel Paul preaches did not originate with human beings. These verses repeat the claim from 1:1—not from men, not by human agency. (This echo of 1:1 may provide support for beginning the new paragraph with v. 11.) On the contrary, Paul received his message by revelation "of Jesus Christ." If the phrase "of Jesus Christ" is subjective genitive, Jesus Christ revealed it to Paul. If it is objective genitive, the revelation was about Jesus Christ. Many translations prefer the former, although vv. 15-16 mention that God revealed his Son. (See my comment at 1:4 concerning the persons of the Godhead working together in the same actions.) In the previous paragraph was a warning against "another gospel." In this paragraph, Paul affirms that his gospel is the genuine gospel.

1:13-17. Paul recounts his former life as a persecutor and destroyer of the church. These things were known to the recipients of the letter. We do not know whether Paul had told them these things on a previous visit, whether the information was well known among the churches, or whether opponents were citing the change in Paul's life as evidence of Paul's duplicity. Formerly, Paul was well-advanced in Judaism (probably a reference to his rabbinical studies), surpassing many other students and zealously following another way of thinking—the traditions of his Jewish ancestors. How does one explain the change in the direction of Paul's life? Paul's answer is that God had acted in

The Independence and Authenticity of Paul's Gospel
Paul was called by God to preach to the Gentiles
He received the gospel by direct revelation from God
He did not consult with other apostles
He was unknown to the Judean churches
He was accepted by the "pillars" in Jerusalem on a later visit

his life (vv. 15-16) to choose him, call him, and to reveal "to him" (literally, "in him") His Son, with the purpose that Paul would preach the gospel message of Jesus to the Gentiles.

1:16-17. After Paul understood God's calling in his life, he did not seek knowledge or input from any human being or from those who were apostles, but went directly to Arabia before returning to Damascus. In the time of Paul, the northern part of Arabia extended almost to the city of Damascus. The text does not say that he was in Arabia three years, only that after three years he went up to Jerusalem. Remember Paul's purpose in this section: to show that he was called by God and received his message directly by revelation from God.

1:18-24. This is the second section in the larger literary unit. Here Paul demonstrates the independence of his gospel. In this section, he notes that even though after three years he went up to Jerusalem for fifteen days, his contacts with leaders of the church on that visit were limited—he saw only Peter and James the brother of the Lord. After that brief visit, he went home (to Cilicia) and did not interact with the churches of Judea.

1:18-19. On this visit to Jerusalem Paul visited Peter with the purpose of getting information from him. The Greek word, *historeo*, translated "to get information," is the word from which we get our word "history." The text literally reads "other of the apostles not I saw, except James the brother of the Lord." The text does not clearly describe James as an apostle. A possible reading is, "I did not see any other of the apostles, but I did see James the brother of the Lord." James was not an apostle in the sense of the Twelve and Matthias (who was selected to replace Judas Iscariot in Acts 1). The word "apostle" (*apostolos*) means "sent one." In the New Testament, various Christians are described as "sent," and the word *apostolos* is rendered in some translations as "apostle" with reference to those who were not among the original Apostles. A good example occurs in 2 Cor. 8:23 where the word is used of messengers or representatives of the churches. For more examples where the word is used not in reference to the original apostles, see Acts 14:4, 14 (Barnabas), Rom. 16:7 (Andronicus and Junias), 1 Cor. 4:9 (Apollos), and Phil. 2:25 (Epaphroditus).

1:20-24. Paul wants to verify the accuracy of his description of his life immediately after becoming a Christian (v. 20). He continues with a description of his travels to Syria and to his home region in Cilicia. It is possible he reverses the order since Acts 9:30 describes his travel to Cilicia and Acts 11:25-26 describes a year in Antioch of Syria. His point hinges on his independence from the original Judean churches—that he was not seeking approval from them, that they were only hearing of his activities on behalf of the gospel, and that they were glorifying God because of Paul.

Galatians 2

[Note: it is suggested that the introductory materials in this guide be reread before beginning a preparatory reading and analysis, and that the five steps of Bible study outlined there be followed.]

CONTENT

The paragraphing included in the Content section of each chapter gives suggestions to help the reader. Each student is encouraged to identify the paragraphs and the subsections within each paragraph as part of his or her own study. In most chapters, the division of the biblical text into paragraphs is fairly standard in modern translations. When significant variations or questions exist, these are noted in these Bible Study Guides.

Outline of the Chapter

2:1-10	A visit to Jerusalem; Paul's apostleship, gospel, and work recognized
2:11-14	Paul rebukes Peter's inconsistency related to the Gentile believers
2:15-21	Paul's gospel

Overview of the Chapter

2:1-14, continues Paul's defense that began in 1:11 (see notes at 1:11-17)

[Note: 2:1-10 contains some interesting and infrequent Greek constructions, but since the meaning is clear and there is general agreement in the translations, these are not explained in detail in this guide]

2:15-21, describes Paul's gospel and introduces the following chapters. Paul foreshadows the accusations that were apparently being raised about his gospel of grace, matters he will consider more fully in the doctrinal section of Chapters 3-4.

Observations about the Contents of the Chapter

Paul continues to show that the gospel he originally preached in Galatia was authentic, and that the changes and additional requirements being preached by some Jewish teachers are not part of the genuine gospel. Here is a quick review: Paul has noted that his gospel came by revelation from Jesus Christ, that his gospel was a part of God's purpose for him, that the gospel took his life in entirely new directions, that his gospel was for the Gentiles, that his gospel was independent, that his gospel was accepted by Christian leaders in Jerusalem, and that his gospel was approved and praised by Christian communities in Judea.

Much later Paul went to Jerusalem again, taking with him Titus, a Gentile believer. The leaders in Jerusalem did not require that Titus be circumcised. When some Christians raised questions about such liberty, in a private meeting with the leaders Paul explained the gospel he was preaching to the Gentiles. The outcome of the meeting was that Paul's gospel to the Gentiles was approved and nothing was added. No other requirements were imposed. The leaders recognized Paul's calling to preach to the Gentiles, just as Peter was preaching to the Jews. In fact, leaders like James, Peter, and John extended full fellowship to Paul, mentioning in addition only the need to keep in mind the needs of the poor.

Another evidence of the independence and validity of Paul's gospel to the Gentiles comes from his encounter with Peter in Antioch. Peter was subtly making a fellowship distinction between Jews and Gentiles—in essence becoming a "men-pleaser"—by allowing himself to be influenced by the presence of some Jews who did not fully accept Gentile believers. Peter's influence was extending to others in Antioch, even to Barnabas. Paul spoke to Peter publicly about the matter. "If you as a Jew can in Christ live like a Gentile, why are the Gentiles in Christ required to live like Jews?"

In the last section of the chapter, Paul summarizes the autobiographical evidence of his independence in the gospel to the Gentiles with a description of his gospel. If justification in Christ is not on the basis of law, no part of the law should be understood as essential. Justification is by faith in Christ. The purpose of the law was to define sin and lawbreaking. God used the law for his purpose and the law was an essential part of that purpose, but that does not make Jesus a servant of sin or a servant of the law. The law actually becomes the cause for leaving the law behind. Paul says it this way: "I died to the law to live for God. I died by being crucified with Christ so Christ could live in me." When one clearly understands how God used the law to usher in his grace, the law does not annul grace, it actually exalts the grace of God. If justification could come by the law, the death of Christ would not be needed. But since justification could never come through the law, the importance of the gospel apart from the law is clearly seen.

STUDY HELPS

2:1-10. "After fourteen years" may refer back (1) to the time of Paul's conversion or (2) to his previous visit to Jerusalem. Paul's point is that he has not had much contact with the church in Jerusalem or with the other apostles. The primary question is whether the "fourteen years" includes the three years previously mentioned in the context, or whether the two references consecutively add to seventeen years. Said another way, the two options for understanding the reference to "fourteen years" place the Jerusalem visit of Galatians 2 either 14 or 17 years after Paul's conversion.

Galatians 1-2:
Probable Timeline of Paul's Early Years as a Christian

30*	Jesus' death
32-33	Paul's conversion to Christianity
35-36	Went up to Jerusalem after three years
49-50	Went to Jerusalem to conference of Acts 15 (same visit described in Gal. 2)

*all dates AD

We can understand the options better by identifying a possible date for Paul's conversion and then adding either 14 years or 17 years. First, if Paul was converted early, in AD 31-33, the Galatians 2 visit occurs around either AD 45-47 or AD 48-50 (perhaps in parallel to the visit in Acts 11:30 or perhaps corresponding to the Jerusalem meeting). Second, if the date of Paul's conversion is seen as a little later (AD 35-36), the Galatians 2 visit is most likely the same visit as that recorded in Acts 15, the Jerusalem assembly in AD 50. (Adding 17 years to the late conversion date does not give a meaningful result.) Paul mentions the presence of Barnabas both in Acts 15 and in Galatians 2. Despite the fact that there are points that must be reconciled, the best option seems to be to place Paul's conversion story in Acts 9 as early as AD 32-33, to understand the 3 years and 14 years as consecutive, and to identify the visit to Jerusalem mentioned in 2:1 with the visit to the Jerusalem meeting in Acts 15. (See "Recipients and Date" in the Introduction for more on the date of the book.)

2:1-3. Paul went up to Jerusalem by revelation (compare 1:12) with Barnabas and Titus, who was a Gentile. In a private meeting with some of the leaders, Paul explained the gospel he was preaching to the Gentiles, apparently to verify that his work among the Gentiles was being recognized. He was not seeking acceptance or approval, although in the context his concern was to show that the gospel he had presented among the Gentiles was a verified gospel that should not be changed. That his message was accepted was shown by the fact that the leaders in Jerusalem did not require the circumcision of Titus. This is especially significant when one recalls that the purpose of the Jerusalem assembly in Acts 15 was to address the question as to whether Gentiles had to submit to circumcision in order to be Christians.

2:4-5. These verses appear to be parenthetical. Notice the smooth transition from v. 3 to v. 6, with a repeated reference to the influential leaders (compare vv. 2, 6). Why had Paul felt it necessary to meet with leaders in Jerusalem? That is, what is the subject of v. 4? In the context, it appears to refer to the fact that Paul's gospel did not include circumcision for the Gentiles. The question arose because of some with false motives or false pretenses, who were "secretly inserted" for the purpose of spying on the freedom proclaimed by Paul (freedom from Jewish rules, including circumcision?) and for the purpose of enslaving (to Judaism, including circumcision?). Consider the literal reading: "⁴ on account of the false brothers secretly brought in, who came in to spy on our freedom which we have in Christ Jesus, in order that they might enslave, ⁵ to whom we gave subjection not even an hour, so the truth of the gospel might remain with you."

Several difficult questions arise in this text. Who secretly inserted these false brothers? Who are they (Jewish Christians, Judaizing teachers)? Where were they inserted (the Antioch church, the Jerusalem church, the Galatians 2 meeting, the Jerusalem meeting of Acts 15)? The answers to such questions may help us understand the larger historical context, but Paul's point is unchanged by such details.

Paul writes that he and those with him did not yield (*eiko*, surrender) to these at all, so that the gospel Paul had proclaimed among the Gentiles (the truth of the gospel) might remain in place with you (the Gentile Christians to whom Paul is writing in the Galatian churches).

2:6-10. The influential leaders (cf. v. 2) were not considered special in God's sight, and they did not change Paul's gospel. Recall Paul's purpose in the context of the book of Galatians: he was showing the independence of the gospel to the Gentiles, the gospel which he had received directly from God.

2:7-8. These verses contain more explanation and parenthetical insertions. Rather than adding anything ("on the contrary"), they (the influential leaders, or those in the meeting) accepted that Paul had been entrusted by God with taking the gospel to the uncircumcised—just as Peter to the circumcised. This description of the Gentiles as "uncircumcised" perhaps accentuates that the Gentiles can become Christians and remain uncircumcised. Both Peter and Paul were empowered (energized) by God as apostles in their respective works.

2:9-10. Paul names three specific church leaders who recognized the work of Paul and Barnabas among the Gentiles. (The James mentioned here is the Lord's brother, not the apostle who was the brother of John.) Since the work of Paul and Barnabas was the result of grace given to them by God, fellowship was extended with an agreement for preaching both to the Gentiles and to the circumcised (note the change of terminology from v. 8), and that Paul remember the poor, which he was eager to do. This reference to the poor could refer to taking the gospel to people of every economic standing, but more likely refers to the needs of the impoverished Christians in Jerusalem. The meaning is that Paul, as he traveled extensively and developed Gentile churches, should remember the needs of the Christians in Jerusalem. This need is mentioned in Acts 11:27-30, and we know that Paul advanced the project among the churches (1 Cor. 16:1-2; 2 Cor. 8:9; Romans 15:25-27; Acts 24:17).

2:11-14. The timing of this visit by Peter to Antioch is not given in the Bible. It is not necessary to see the events of Galatians 2 as chronological, since Paul is simply recounting various evidences of his independence in the gospel message. If the events are seen as chronological, the Galatians 2 visit is better identified with an earlier visit to Jerusalem, since the encounter with Peter would seem out of place after the decision reached in Acts 15.

2:11-12. Paul's purpose is to show that his gospel was not dependent on the apostles. Paul opposed Peter personally because Peter was wrong. Paul describes Peter's hypocrisy of eating with (accepting) Gentile believers before some Jewish believers arrived from Jerusalem (from James). (Again, this is James the brother of Jesus. James has already been identified as in agreement with Paul's ministry and gospel [v. 9], so the purpose of the reference in the context is unclear with a chronological reading, thus lending support to the idea that the events described in Galatians 2 are not presented chronologically.) Once the visitors arrived, Peter quit eating with the Gentiles (he separated himself) because of fear of the circumcision (perhaps "circumcision party" gives a clearer meaning). This issue was not only circumcision. This text shows that the restrictions some Jewish Christians were placing on the Gentiles extended to points of fellowship such as eating together, and perhaps to other items based in the Law of Moses. The question was not only whether Gentiles had to be circumcised; the question also had to do with their obligation to maintain other requirements of the Law.

2:13-14. Other Jews (Jewish Christians) followed Peter in this hypocrisy, including Barnabas. Such actions were inconsistent (literally, "they were not walking straight") with the gospel Paul was defending and explaining (the truth of the gospel, compare 2:5). Paul spoke to Peter "before all." Paul confronted Peter in the presence of those already mentioned in the passage. Whether "all" must be extended to include others of the church at Antioch is not clear from the passage. The meaning of Paul's statement to Peter is this: "If you as a Jewish Christian recognize that you are free to live as a Gentile without all of the restrictions of the Law and that you do not have to live like a Jew, why are you trying to put on the Gentiles require-ments that you do not put on yourself?" Literally, "how are you requiring the Gentiles to Judaize?" This verbal infinitive form appears only here in the New Testament.

2:15-21. Although the connection between these verses and the previous section is apparent, it seems better to treat this as a sep-arate, summarizing paragraph because the principles set forth apply more broadly than to the specific situation with Peter in 2:11-14. It is unlikely that 2:15-21 is a continuation of Paul's conversation with Peter. The question is, "Who are the 'we' of vv. 15-17?"

2:15-16. "Even we who are Jews by nature and are not sinners from among the Gentiles," even we recognize that justi-fication is not by works of the law but by the faith of Jesus Christ. In Greek, the word "law" is anarthrous (without the definite ar-ticle), but is clearly a reference to the Law of Moses. However, the principle would apply more broadly to any legal system, that is, any system based on law-keeping. In the context, Paul is re-ferring to Jewish Christians. Jewish Christians understand that justification is not by the law but is by Christ. In fact, justifica-tion by the law is impossible (v. 16b). Justification is possible only through the faith of Christ Jesus, by the faith of Christ (2:16), for those who believe in Christ. While it is possible to interpret the phrase "of Christ" as objective genitive (faith in Christ), in this text and in many others (Rom. 3:22, 26; Gal. 2:20, 3:22; Eph. 3:12; Phil. 3:9) it seems better to understand a subjec-tive genitive (faith of Christ, the faithfulness of Christ to God's will and purpose). This point is explained in more detail in my Bible Study Guide for Romans (see Chapter 3).

2:17-21. Since justification by the law is impossible, all are sinners under the law. It is also true that all are sinners, even while they are seeking justification in Christ. When such is the case (as it always is, the first class condition reflects reality), does that make Christ an agent (minister) of sin? May it never be! With a little patience, one can follow Paul's reasoning in this text, even though it may be a little obscure at first reading. "What I once destroyed" in the context is a reference to the Christian faith. As a Christian, Paul is seeking to build up what he formerly sought to destroy. He illustrates the point of v. 17. All are sinners (transgressors), whether they are defined as such by the law, or whether the fact is to be assumed because they are seeking justification in Christ. The argument is built sequentially with the continued use of "for" in the larger context.

2:19-21. Note the parallel construction: through the law (through trying to keep the law), Paul became dead to the law, and through Christ (seeking justification in Christ) he became dead (was crucified). In dying to the law (v. 19) he was free to live to God. In being crucified with Christ (v. 20), he was free to live through Christ living in him. (See Paul's parallel to vv. 19-20 in Romans 6:1-23; 7:1-6). In Paul's gospel, life is lived not through the efforts of the Christian (it is no longer I who live) but through Christ living within the Christian. Life is lived in the flesh but is by the faith (faithfulness) of Christ who lives in the Christian. (See Matt. 28:20; John 14:23; Rom. 8:10; Eph. 3:17 and Col. 1:27 for other New Testament references to the presence and indwelling of Christ within the Christian.)

The Parallelism of Galatians 2:19-20

19—Through the law
    I died to the law
        To live to God
20—With Christ
    I have been crucified
        To live, not I but Christ in me

2:21. In the gospel that Paul proclaims, he does not nullify the grace of God. Rather, he accentuates God's grace. Since righteousness (*dikaiosune*, justification) cannot come through law, Christ's death was necessary for justification. Paul says it this way: "If righteousness can come through the law (which it cannot!), Christ's death is meaningless. That would set aside

God's grace. The only way to God is through the faith of Christ (Christ's faithfulness in doing the saving work God sent him to do). If relationship with God is possible in any other way, Christ died for nothing." Proclaiming such a message surely calls attention to the supremacy of grace!

In 2:15-21 is the climax of Paul's argument in favor of his gospel. The last verses of the chapter (2:15-21) provide a transition to the doctrinal section of Chapters 3-4, bridging from Paul's autobiographical references to an explanation of the importance of the teachings that undergird the authentic gospel.

Galatians 3

[Note: it is suggested that the introductory materials in this guide be read before beginning your own preparatory reading and analysis, especially if the reader is not yet familiar with the five-step Bible study process.]

CONTENT

The paragraphing and outline included in the Content section of each chapter are only suggestions. The student is encouraged to read the biblical text carefully to identify the paragraphs and the subsections within each paragraph to assist in his or her own study. After identifying the paragraphs, the student may want to try to summarize the content or message of each paragraph by developing paragraph headings or titles.

Outline of the Chapter

3:1-14   Law or faith
    3:1-5   The experience of the Galatians
    3:6-9   Abraham's example of faith apart from law
    3:10-14   The curse of the law
3:15-22   The law and the promise, the purpose of the law
3:23-29   Inheritance as sons of God comes through the
                 promise by faith
Note: the larger paragraph likely continues through 4:7, but in this guide the chapter division is being honored and the larger paragraph is divided into two shorter but related paragraphs.

Overview of the Chapter

Chapters 3-4 are often described as the doctrinal section of Galatians. As noted previously, the summary in 2:15-21 provides a transition to Chapters 3-4. These chapters must be understood against the background of that summary.

The Galatians became Christians by faith, not by following the law. That is not hard to understand when one considers that the promise and Abraham's example of faith preceded the law. Faith is exercised apart from the law. In fact, the purpose of the law was to point to the future fulfillment of the promise. When the promise was fulfilled, the law was no longer needed.

Observations about the Contents of the Chapter

In the doctrinal summary of 2:15-21, Paul has provided a bridge from his own experience, and from the validity and independence of the gospel he preached to the Gentiles, to a more extended treatment of the gospel—that justification is by faith and not by observance of the law.

To focus the question, Paul begins this chapter by raising several rhetorical questions. In every case, the answer is "by belief," pointing to the necessity of faith. Abraham's example of faith preceded by over four centuries the giving of the law through Moses and was therefore obviously independent of the law. Further, the promise to Abraham about a "blessing on the nations" is evidence that the Old Testament Scriptures foresaw the inclusion of the Gentiles on the basis of faith. Such justification can never be on the basis of law, because perfect observance of the law is impossible, so that the law and human efforts to keep the law ultimately become a source of curses rather than blessings. About 1500 years after Abraham and 1000 years after Moses, God mentioned this again when his prophet Haggai said that the righteous live by faith. Christ made it possible for everyone—both Jews and Gentiles—to escape the curse of the law.

God's promise to Abraham can never be changed because it is a confirmed covenant. The promise extended to many descendants of Abraham, but God specifically mentioned that the promise would be fulfilled through Abraham's seed—singular not plural. God was referring specifically to the coming of Christ. Inheritance cannot be both by law and by promise. It is either by promise, or it is by law. If it is by promise, which it clearly is, then it cannot be by law.

What good was the law? What was the purpose of the law? The law was temporary, lasting until the Christ (Messiah) should come. The law was not opposed to the promise of God; in fact, it pointed to and led to Christ. Once Christ came, faith in Christ also came, and the law was no longer needed.

Therefore, the inheritance as sons of God comes through faith in Christ Jesus when in baptism the believer puts on Christ. Status as sons erases all of the distinctions that formerly excluded some from sonship. In Christ, sonship is not only for Jews, it is also for Gentiles. Sonship is not only for freemen, it is also for slaves. Sonship is not only for males, it is also for females. Everyone in Christ is now seed of Abraham and an heir according to the promise--therefore not according to the law.

STUDY HELPS
3:1-5. The description "foolish" is literally "unthinking" (not + mind, *anoetas*). "Bewitched" used in a figurative sense means deceived. Paul is urging a careful consideration of the false teachings of the Judaizers. Jesus Christ has been publicly proclaimed (*prographo*, literally, written before, set forth on a public placard or billboard) as crucified. The word sometimes referred to the posting of an official legal notice. This is a reference to Paul's teaching and his emphasis on Jesus Christ. Paul publicly and openly proclaimed Jesus Christ. The Galatians were turning away from what had been made known to them in the preaching of the gospel.

Paul focuses the contrast with a series of questions (vv. 2-5). Did you receive the Spirit through works of law or by faith? Are you foolish (compare v. 1)? Would you begin with the Spirit and try to finish with the flesh (that is, by human effort)? Have you suffered so much for nothing? Does God give the Spirit and work miracles through your works of law or through your faith?

3:3-5. In accepting and following the teaching of the Judaizing teachers, the Galatians were trying to fulfill their Christian commitment by keeping the Mosaic Law. The meaning of "suffering" is not clear in the context. Perhaps the reference is to persecution by the Jews, perhaps to their exclusion by some Jewish Christians, or perhaps to the doubt and upheaval in their faith. The churches established by Paul on his first missionary journey undoubtedly suffered as a result of their decision to follow Jesus. As these churches were established, Paul and those with him were persecuted; Paul was even stoned and left for dead. When Paul and his companions decided to visit the churches again, their purpose is described as "strengthening the souls of the disciples, encouraging them to continue in the faith, and saying that through many tribulations we must enter the kingdom of God" (Acts 14:21-23). Given this background, the message of Paul in vv. 3-5 is something like this: "You previously endured many things. Is God's provision (of the Spirit) so incomplete that you now have to supplement it?"

3:6-9. The example of Abraham is an example of the power of faith. Abraham believed God and it was credited to him as righteousness (Gen. 15:6; Ps. 32:1). Therefore, believers (those who are "of the faith") are sons of Abraham—that is, they have the same faith nature. Paul sees in Gen. 12:3 and Gen. 18:18 references to God's justification of the Gentiles by faith, something Paul calls a proclamation of the gospel ahead of time (v. 8). The gospel to which Paul refers is the blessing of God upon all nations (Gentiles). Thus, those who believe (those who are from faith) will be blessed with the believer Abraham. Following the question of vv. 1-5 (law or faith?), Paul's first response is to give an example of faith.

3:10-14. Paul's second response to the question of vv. 1-5 (law or faith?) is to explain what happens to those who rely on works of law. Such people are under a curse because no one keeps the law completely. Paul cites Deut. 27:26 to prove the point. The Old Testament law becomes the declaration of unrighteousness and the cause of a curse. Paul made the same claim in 2:16—no one will be justified by works of the law. On the contrary, the just or righteous person lives by faith (Hab. 2:4).

    3:12. In v. 12, Paul returns to the possible exception— something that is in reality an impossibility. The law is not based on faith; only the one who does all of the works of the law perfectly will live by those works. The problem is that the Old Testament is a clear declaration of human inability to keep the law. This is why God, in the gospel preached by Paul, opens a new way to justification, not by law but by faith. Christ redeems from the curse of the law by becoming a curse for humanity, a curse declared and fulfilled in Paul's citation of Deut. 21:23: "cursed is everyone who hangs on a tree."

3:14. Finally, Paul says that the redemption accomplished by Christ allows the Gentiles to receive the blessing promised to Abraham, so that all by faith receive the promise of the Spirit. The promise to Abraham results in blessing on the nations. The promise by faith points to the Spirit.

3:15-22. To explain the relationship between the law and the promise, and the purpose of the law, Paul introduces an example from everyday life (literally, I speak according to man). Paul illustrates by using the example of a will that controls an inheritance. The illustration is taken from the legal realm. Once the covenant (*diatheke,* agreement, will) is ratified or confirmed, it cannot be annulled. (The argument in this passage is similar to Heb. 9:15-20).

3:16-18. In these verses is Paul's response to the idea set forth by the Judaizing teachers that the Mosaic Law had superseded or replaced the promise to Abraham. The promise to Abraham was duly ratified (Gen. 15:12-21) and thus cannot be set aside. "Promises" (v. 16) may be plural because of the number of times the promise was repeated, or it may reflect the various facets of the promise (blessing on the nations, the promised seed, innumerable descendants).

Paul's argument turns on the use of the singular "seed" referring to a descendant. Paul makes the reference apply to Jesus (not Isaac and not Israel). The promise is thus completely disconnected from the law. Paul makes his point even clearer (v. 17): the law was given 430 years after the promise; therefore, it cannot cancel God's ratification of the promise and it cannot invalidate (*katargeo*, annul) the promise. The promise has priority. The basis of the inheritance has not been transferred to the law so that the promise is no longer the basis of the inheritance. The inheritance was given to Abraham through the promise. The promise to Abraham is still the basis of inheritance.

3:19-22. The logical questions that follow are these: "What then is the purpose of the law?" and "Is the law against the promises of God?" To answer the first question, Paul says in v. 19 that the law was added because of transgressions, that it was temporary until the seed should come, and that it was administered by angels through an intermediary. These truths show the inferiority of the law in comparison to the promise. The promise was given at God's initiative, is eternal, and was given to Abraham directly from God.

3:20. An intermediary is needed only if there is more than one party. The context suggests that the promise was given unilaterally and did not depend on an intermediary. The promise was given directly from God to Abraham, without mediation. Paul thus shows the superiority of the promise to the law.

3:21-22. The second question (v. 21) is whether the law worked against God's promises. Paul repeats his previous negative response: May it never be! Paul proceeds to show how the law was actually pointing toward the ultimate fulfillment of the promise. Here is his line of reasoning: If a law able to give life had been given (second class condition, contrary to fact, meaning that such a law was not given), righteousness could have come by law (impossible because the condition cannot be met). On the contrary, the Old Testament (scripture) imprisoned the whole world (literally, all things) under sin. In this way, the law opened the way for the promise to function as God intended, as a blessing to the whole world. The promise was given to all who believe because of the faith of Christ (cf. 2:16).

Paraphrase of Galatians 3:26-29

Now all of you are sons of God through faith in Christ Jesus, because all of you were baptized into Christ and therefore are clothed with Christ. Since you are all "sons," it does not matter whether you are Jew or Gentile, slave or free, male or female. As sons, you are all one, so you can all belong to Christ, be descendants of Abraham, and as sons be heirs according to the promise.

3:23-29. The final section of the chapter shows why being sons of God (compare 3:7) and heirs of the promise depends on faith. Paul has just said (v. 22) that the Scripture (*graphe*, writing) includes (*sugkleio*, shuts up, encloses, imprisons, thus figuratively "concludes") all under sin, so that the promise (*epangelia*, message, announcement) out of faith in Christ Jesus will be given to all who believe. Under the law all were held as prisoners (v. 22) until the coming of faith. Paul argues that the law was in effect before faith came (not the faith of Abraham, but in the context, faith in Christ Jesus). Paul describes the role of the law before the coming of faith as one of guardian *(paidagogos,* custodian, tutor, perhaps parallel to the contemporary idea of a "nanny" but in the context the word is masculine), preparing all people to be declared righteous by faith. When faith comes and brings full sonship, the guardian is no longer needed.

3:26-27. In Christ Jesus, all are sons of God through faith. In the context, the use of "sons" rather than "children" is intentional. Sons are heirs. Becoming sons of God is associated with baptism into Christ. Paul's purpose is not to set in place another human work, but to indicate the nature of responsive obedient faith. In the passage, baptism is the method of becoming a Christian, thereby becoming a son of God, and in the context, becoming also an heir of God. Given the entire context, baptism in this passage is not metaphorical and it is not a work. Paul clearly associates it with faith, it is a response based on faith. In baptism, one is clothed with Christ.

3:28-29. These verses make clear that the barriers that formerly excluded some and included others are removed. This does not mean that there are no longer any distinctions such as Jew or Greek, slave or free, male and female. The distinctions remain, but in determining who has the right to be a Christian (son, heir) by faith, there are no barriers. The barriers mentioned were significant in Judaism. Only sons could inherit, daughters could not. Only free men had rights to inherit, slaves did not. In the Jewish system, Gentiles could not inherit. Reading these verses in the context clarifies the application. These factors (male or female, free or slave, Jew or Gentile) no longer decide who can and who cannot approach God by faith—because all are "sons." These distinctions are not a part of salvation. All are one in Christ Jesus; all belong to Christ; all are descendants of Abraham; all are heirs according to the promise. This encompasses and summarizes all that Paul has set forth in the chapter and sets the stage for the continuation of the thought in 4:1-7.

Because this passage is often used as a prooftext and is quoted out of context, it is worth noting that this passage says nothing about roles, responsibilities, qualifications, and participation in various activities—in the home, in the church, or in the culture. The point is that becoming an heir of God in Christ is not based on the distinctions that characterized Judaism.

Galatians 4

CONTENT

The paragraphing included in the Content section of each chapter provides suggestions or guides to help with understanding the construction of the text and the development of the message. The student is encouraged to identify the paragraphs (and sub-sections within each paragraph) as part of his or her own study. Once again in this chapter, the division into paragraphs of the biblical text in this chapter is fairly standard in modern translations, except see the note in the outline below.

Outline of the Chapter

4:1-7   Sons and therefore heirs of God
            (continuation of thought from 3:21-29)
Note: concerning 4:8-11, some outlines include these verses with 1-7, others with 12-20.
4:8-20   Paul's concern for the Galatians, a personal appeal
4:21-31   Allegory of Hagar and Sarah

Overview of the Chapter
        As reflected in the outline, this chapter is fairly consistently divided into three sections. Some would identify the first two sections as vv. 1-7, 8-20; others as vv. 1-11, 12-20. The content of vv. 8-11 provides a smooth transition so that one can see the possibility of including it with either the preceding or the succeeding section.
        Verses 21-31 contain an allegory, described as such by the author (v. 24). Allegory is a type of extended metaphor and identifies a new application or lesson in past events, a meaning that has no relation to the meaning of the original author. Allegory identifies persons or events as symbols or representations that go beyond the original intent of the passage. The use of

allegory is difficult, and the modern student of the Bible must be careful about assigning an allegorical meaning to a passage. In this case, the inspired author identifies the allegory, thus giving it validity. Allegory begins in the present and looks backward to identify symbols where they are not customarily seen; typology begins in the past and looks forward so that certain aspects of Christian faith are prefigured or symbolized in the Old Testament. Typology is anticipatory when seen from the viewpoint of the original 'type' and is fulfillment-oriented when seen from the viewpoint of the subsequent 'antitype.' Typology is generally more dependent on similarities than is allegory. The parallelism in allegory may not touch every point of the comparison. Many parables have an allegorical aspect (parable of the trees, Judges 9; the vine, Psalm 80, Isaiah 5; Nathan's prophecy against David, 2 Samuel 12; some of Jesus' parables).

Observations about the Contents of the Chapter

In this case, the chapter division does not mark the beginning of a new thought or subject since the first verses of this chapter continue the thought from 3:21-29. In 4:1-7, the information about sons, heirs, seed, erasing lines of exclusion, and completing God's promise (presented in 3:21-29) is applied. When the son is young, it may be hard to tell the difference between the son and the slave child of about the same age. This is because the son is overseen by guardians until he reaches the age of maturity. At first the son looks a lot like the slave child, but over time the difference becomes obvious. The explanation helps us understand the illustration. Jesus came to give freedom from slavery, to do the Father's will, to redeem from the curse of the law, and to give full sonship to all. One evidence of this is that God sent his Spirit by which we now know God as Father. We are no longer slaves but sons, and because we are sons, God has made us heirs.

Paul is very concerned about the Galatians because rejecting the authentic gospel means rejecting the privileges of sonship and returning to a status as slaves. It means going back to trying to observe details of the law that one can never satisfactorily keep and that can never bring justification and relationship with God.

Paul calls on his personal relationship with the Galatians as motivation to continue in the gospel he had preached to them. The other (Judaizing) teachers have ulterior motives. Paul reminds the Galatians of how he came among them in weakness and illness, how they accepted him, and how he sought their good.

Finally, as though to clinch his point, Paul presents an allegory based on the Hagar and Sarah story to show that God's purpose has always been to provide inheritance through freedom and not through bondage. Hagar and Sarah, and several other aspects of the Old Testament history, are figures to represent two covenants, two cities, and the contrast between the promise and the law.

STUDY HELPS

4:1-7. "But I say" is a way to continue and expand the previous point (3:21-29). Here is another illustration from everyday life, applied to those who are sons and heirs of God according to the promise (3:29).

4:1-2. The heir (son), while he is a small child still too young to take responsibility for his own affairs, is placed under guardians and stewards until the date set by his father. This phrase, "the date set by his father," is reflected in 4:4 when God sends Jesus at the appropriate time. While the heir remains in the status described (overseen and controlled by others), he is not different from a slave even though he is the (eventual) owner of everything. Paul has previously described the law as a guardian (3:24). Therefore, this section should be seen as an explanation of that point. Paul is describing the status of those under the law.

4:3. As children (minors, immature), we (primarily the Jews under the law before the coming of Christ, but see comment below concerning a possible application to the Gentiles) were enslaved to elemental things (*stoikeion*) of the world. This phrase focuses on the status as children. The Bible uses this idea of "elemental things" in various ways: (1) a child's early training and basic teachings (Heb. 5:12; 6:1); (2) the basic elements of the physical creation (2 Pet. 3:10, 12); and (3) elementary understandings (Col. 2:8, 20). The first option provides the clearest application in this passage.

The Jews under the law (and perhaps the Gentiles also functioning under a "law system" as described in Rom. 2:14-16) had a status as children with regard to the promise, because they had not yet reached maturity and therefore had not yet inherited. While both Jews and Gentiles may be in view, in the context the primary application is to the Jews to show that the purpose of the Old Testament law was to point to Christ. The Law as custodian was focused on basics and could not move beyond the elementary understandings to see the purpose of the Law in God's eternal will.

4:4-5. At the right time (fullness, *pleroma,* of time, cf. 4:2), God sent his Son. Commentators have noted that the first century was the right time due to the Pax Romana (Roman peace), ease of travel on the Roman road system, and the presence of koine (common) Greek as a common language. "Born of woman" may focus on Christ's humanity or may point back to and accentuate 3:28. "Born under the Law" shows that Jesus was born in the context of the Law and was himself subject to the elemental things. Jesus, born under the law and participant in the law, was uniquely qualified to redeem those under the law (the phrase is repeated in 4:4 and 4:5, both times without the article, simply "law" but clearly referring to the Old Testament law). God bought back (redeemed) those under the law (Jews) so they could be adopted as sons.

Paul's purpose in this section is to describe how and why the Jews are given access to justification in Christ, since all believers are heirs of Abraham through the faith of Christ.

4:6-7. Those who are sons (and heirs) receive special blessings. These verses declare that God sends the Spirit of his Son into the hearts of his sons. God sent his Son (4:4); God sends the Spirit of his Son (4:6). These affirmations demonstrate that the believer is part of a spiritual family with intimate relationship as a son (reflected in the cry 'Abba'), and accentuate that the believer is not a slave but a son and an heir.

4:8-11. These verses are treated separately here due to the question about whether they should be included in the previous paragraph (with vv. 1-7) or the subsequent paragraph (vv. 12-20). The application of the first verse (v. 8) is not obvious. Is Paul continuing his description of the Jews, or is this a description of the Gentiles in their former separation from God? In this passage, Paul describes those who formerly did not know God and were enslaved to beings that by nature are not gods at all. What it would mean that the Jews did not know God is perhaps hard to understand, although the word translated "know" describes intimate relationship—something the Jews had lost in their focus on the law. The phrase "not gods" is often a description of idols, although it is also possible that Paul is using the phrase, the "elemental things" (*stoikeion*, see v. 3, and also v. 9 where the same Greek word is used again) to refer to the law which had become an idol in the sense that loyalty to the law had replaced loyalty to God. The reference in v. 3 is to the law, the repetition of the same Greek word in v. 9 can be understood in the same sense.

The "now" of v. 9 is in contrast to the "then" of v. 8. Some of the Galatian Christians (likely referring to the Gentiles, but possibly referring to Jewish Christians) were apparently accepting the false gospel of the Judaizers. Paul describes this acceptance as a process of turning back again to the elemental things. To return to the law is to return to elemental things, as described in v. 3. If the phrase is applied to the Gentiles, the idea is that of moving from the slavery of paganism to the slavery of legalism devoted to the law. Applied to the Jews, the idea is that of moving back into the slavery of legalism devoted to the law, having formerly escaped it through belief in Christ. Regardless of the application to Jews, to Gentiles, or to both, in v. 10 Paul describes a slavish regard for certain special days, months, seasons, and years. Paul is afraid that if the false gospel of the Judaizers is accepted in the churches of Galatia, his efforts to present the authentic gospel to the Gentiles whether in Galatia or in other places will be hindered, and the genuine gospel will be emptied of its power. He describes this possibility as "having labored in vain."

4:12-20. In this paragraph, Paul expresses his concern for the Galatians and makes a personal appeal. Verse 12 is difficult to understand, probably because it is a reference to a specific matter known to the Galatian churches but not to the modern reader. Without deciding whether Paul's reference is to viewpoints, to shared experiences past or present, or to other aspects of the relationship, what is clear is that this is Paul's call to mutuality, reflected in the direct address, "brothers." The last phrase of v. 12 probably refers to the fact that during his visit to them they accepted him and his message. This understanding connects the last part of v. 12 with vv. 13-15.

4:13-16. In reminding the Galatians of their shared past, Paul gives several details concerning his visit to them. He preached the gospel to them despite his illness or infirmity (weakness of the flesh, apparently referring to a physical malady). "At the first" can be translated "formerly" and does not necessarily imply a second. The Bible contains other references to Paul's physical problems (see 2 Cor. 12:1-10) and various possibilities have been conjectured. That Paul suffered from a problem with his eyes is one of the better options. The Galatians had not rejected Paul because of his physical condition but had welcomed him beyond what he had expected or hoped. "What has changed?" (Literally, where then is your happiness, v. 15.) Formerly, the relationship between Paul and the Galatians had been very warm. Some see in the reference of v. 15 support for the idea that Paul's physical ailment was some eye problem or disease. Why the radical change of attitude? Why is Paul now an enemy? Is it because he told them the truth?

4:17-18. These verses are not easy to interpret. The unstated subject of v. 17 would seem to be the false teachers. What does "they are zealous of you not well" mean? "Not well" may be translated "not sincerely." Paul sees through the selfish motives of the false teachers. Paul's meaning is something like this:

> The zeal of the Judaizers toward the Galatians is not good, because in fact the false teachers are seeking to exclude the Galatians. Paul says the reason for this is to make the Galatians jealous, that is, so the Galatians will want to reestablish relationship with the false teachers.

4:18-20. "It is good to be jealous for a good thing." What is the subject? This could be a reference to the Judaizers—being jealous for something is good if the motives or purpose are good. In view of the phrase that follows the statement, it is more likely a reference to the Galatians—you were jealous for me and the gospel when I was with you, and it is good to be jealous for these same things in my absence. The Galatians had done an about face in Paul's absence and had developed hostility in place of concern.

Paul expresses his concern for the Galatians by noting the tenderness of the relationship (children) and the depth of his feelings (as childbirth). He desires their growth—that Christ be formed in them, and he longs to be with them and to assure them of the depth of his love and concern with tenderness. "Change my voice" likely means something like "change or soften my tone of voice." Paul's attitude is in obvious contrast to that of the false teachers. Paul is at his wit's end. He does not know what else to do in face of the situation among the Galatian churches.

4:21-31. Paul appeals to them through an allegory. If you are so anxious to be under the law, would it not be good to listen to the law? "Under the law" points back to vv. 4-5. This is the concluding paragraph of the doctrinal section and is built upon the concepts of seed, descendants, sons and heirs in Chapters 3-4.

4:22-26. The details Paul sets forth to develop the allegory are straightforward and easily understood historically. The two sons of Abraham are contrasted, one being born according to the flesh (naturally) and the other according to the promise (supernaturally). The mothers of the two sons are the slave woman and the free woman, Hagar and Sarah, representing two covenants. Hagar represents Mount Sinai and brings forth slave children corresponding to physical Jerusalem. Judaism in Paul's day was centered in Jerusalem. By contrast, Sarah represents the heavenly Jerusalem and the freedom of sonship.

Paul's point is that the promise was never fulfilled in the experience of Israel under the Old Testament. Paul is not saying that the Jews were descendants of Hagar or Ishmael. This is an allegory. The Jews are "like" the experience of Hagar and Ishmael. The believers in Christ are sons of God by the promise "like" the experience of Sarah and Isaac.

4:27-31. This verse (v. 27) quotes Isa. 54:1. Paul's application of the allegory is that believers in Christ are the true descendants of Abraham by the promise and by faith, just like Isaac. During the lifetimes of Ishmael and Isaac, there was enmity and persecution; that is still the case, allegorically speaking. Those seeking to follow God naturally (according to physical descent in Judaism) are persecuting those who seek to follow God by the Spirit. Paul then uses a citation from Gen. 21:10 to say that those who are like the slave woman cannot share the inheritance of the son of the free woman. The verse cited also suggests that the Galatians should throw out the false teachers. The conclusion: Christians are not children of the slave woman but are children of the free woman.

Definition of Allegory

A representation of an abstract or spiritual meaning through concrete or material forms; figurative treatment of one subject under the guise of another. --Dictionary.com

---

The Allegory of 4:21-31

What remains in the study of this section is to make sense of the allegory and to understand how it contributes to Paul's message about a proper definition of the gospel and the demands of the gospel.

Paul's point is that the gospel of salvation is received through faith by grace. The final piece of his argument is an allegory. An allegory takes a historical event and presents it as the vehicle to illustrate and carry a parallel present truth. It is sometimes compared to the type and antitype analogies in the book of Hebrews, although allegory and typology function differently and are based on differing perspectives. This is the only passage identified as an allegory in the New Testament.

An allegory does not prove the truth of a point. This allegory, which uses the Abraham and Sarah story, is Paul's way of illustrating his teaching. One can easily allegorize or spiritualize a text, yet be wrong about the application and miss what the text says or means. The allegory does not prove the truth of Paul's position. The allegory illustrates Paul's point, demonstrating that God has operated in a certain way previously and is doing the same thing again. When we study church history, we learn that the early church went into apostasy by allegorizing and proof-texting their religion through the use of unrelated passages. Untold errors can be taught while quoting the Bible. Allegory is not a way to discover truth. Only divinely inspired allegories can be considered as authoritative applications.

One can describe an allegory as an extended metaphor. An allegory is more than a word or phrase; it uses an entire story. Allegories were developed about the 6th c. BC to avoid anthropomorphisms and crude literalisms which were considered offensive to the Greek mind.

Paul's use of the story has three sections: the facts of the story, an interpretation of the story, and the contemporary application of the story. **First**, the story is set forth briefly in 4:21-23. The focus is on the different origins of the sons. One was naturally born, the other was born by promise. Other contrasts could be noted but they are not the point of Paul's allegory. **Second**, Paul interprets the facts of the allegory by outlining the figurative meanings (4:24-27). The two women represent two covenants. The Sinai covenant (represented by Hagar) bears children who will be slaves. Paul expands the first half of the interpretation by connecting Hagar to the literal Mount Sinai, corresponding to the present city of Jerusalem. This connection appears to depend upon Mt. Sinai as a historic center of Judaism and Jerusalem as the current center of Judaism. **Finally**, Paul observes that the earthly Jerusalem experiences slavery as do also her children.

The contrasts can be set forth in a chart:

Hagar (slave)	Sarah (free)
Ishmael (origin-natural, fleshly)	Isaac (origin-promise, Spirit)
Old Covenant	New Covenant
Law	Promise/gospel/faith/grace
Sinai, physical Jerusalem, Judaism	Jerusalem above, Christianity
Slavery and no inheritance	Sonship and inheritance

To conclude, Paul applies the allegory to the Galatians' experience (4:28-30). The heavenly Jerusalem is free and is the mother of Christians who are identified with Isaac and are born by promise. Just as the two sons were in conflict with the ordinary son pursuing the promise or "spirit" son, so the conflict continues. Abraham expelled the slave woman and her son so that neither she nor her son would share in the inheritance which was reserved only for the son of the free woman. Paul uses the story of Abraham's treatment of Sarah and Hagar, Isaac and Ishmael, to conclude that Judaism and its resultant "slavery" is no longer valid. Christians are called to liberty by the gospel of faith which is the ultimate fulfillment of the promise. To revert to a system that enslaved made no sense to Paul.

Galatians 5

[Note: it is suggested that the introductory materials in this guide be read before beginning your own preparatory reading and analysis.]

CONTENT

The paragraphing and outline included in the Content section of each chapter are only suggestions. The student is encouraged to identify the paragraphs and subsections within each paragraph as part of his or her own study. Your own study Bible will be helpful in this task. In this chapter, modern translations are in agreement concerning the division of the biblical text into paragraphs.

Outline of the Chapter
5:1-15   Christian freedom
5:16-26   Walking in the Spirit

Overview of the Chapter

Chapters 5-6 are sometimes described as the practical section of Galatians. The preferred division of the book identifies three sections of two chapters each—autobiographical, doctrinal, and practical.

To combat the "too hard" gospel that sought to place additional demands from Judaism on the Gentile Christians in the Galatian churches, and to avoid the "too easy" gospel of license, Paul sets forth what it means in a practical way to live as one justified by grace through the faith of Jesus. I refer to this as the "just right" gospel.

The two extremes—the "too hard" gospel and the "too easy" gospel are both reflected in Galatians 5. Verses 1-12 deal with the temptation to legalism, and vv. 13-15 deal with a perverted understanding of Christian freedom that results in license.

Paul's gospel is a call to freedom that is expressed by love and service. Christian freedom is evidenced by a life controlled by the Holy Spirit.

Observations about the Contents of the Chapter

Paul now leaves behind the doctrinal considerations that he has presented in Chapters 3-4. A correct understanding of doctrine set forth in Galatians (1) shows that the Old Testament Scriptures were always pointing to Christ, and (2) accentuates the need to take the gospel to the Gentiles independent of any requirements of the law. The "too hard" gospel that adds requirements from the law is to be rejected. The "just right" gospel that uses the law to point to Christ has always been a part of God's plan. The "too soft" gospel that leads to license must be avoided.

Christ came to bring freedom. That freedom can never be obtained by going back to the burdens of the law and a status as slaves, the situation that Paul has described in various ways in the previous two chapters. Circumcision has no value; if circumcision is given value, Christ has no value. Observing the law is an overwhelming challenge because the entire law must be kept, and keeping the whole law perfectly is an impossible task. Further, there is no place for grace in the legal system. Faith brings hope, justification (righteousness), and the Spirit. Love is evidenced in life, and shows how faith works.

Why would you go back? You were called to freedom; that freedom will allow you to escape the sinful tendencies that the law always arouses. In fact, the Judaizing teachers are showing you exactly where their teaching leads—look at how they bite and destroy. The same thing will happen to you if you accept their altered version of the gospel.

The new life in Christ depends on living in the Spirit. This is how to get rid of the old way of life once and for all.

STUDY HELPS

5:1-15. The first verse of the chapter is sometimes included as part of the final paragraph of Chapter 4, serving as a summary of what Paul has previously written. In this study guide, we are maintaining the chapter divisions as much as possible. "For freedom" suggests purpose; it is also possible to understand the phrase as "with freedom" or "by freedom." Regardless of the option chosen, freedom comes from Christ. Freedom in Christ is wonderfully liberating. Freedom in Christ helps us stand firm and delivers from the slavery that was the result of Judaism.

5:2-3. The construction, "I, Paul," may communicate authority (compare 1:1, as an apostle?). Paul begins by setting forth his point: if you submit to circumcision and seek God's justification through the requirements of Judaism, Christ is of no benefit (literally, profits you nothing). The problem goes beyond the question of circumcision. Circumcision is only an evidence of the Judaizers' dependence on keeping Jewish law in order to be a Christian. The question is, "how one is justified before God?" Circumcision cannot be included as a requirement for Christian faithfulness, because keeping one part of the Jewish law (circumcision, for example) requires that a person keep the whole law (compare Gal. 3:10, also James 2:10).

5:4. You who try to be justified by the law are estranged (*katargeo*, alienated, cut off, separated) from Christ. This verb is also used in 3:17 and 5:11. The KJV renders the verb in the phrase, Christ is become "of no effect." This translation reflects the basic meaning of "powerless, unproductive, unprofitable, empty, or void." To seek justification (righteousness) by the law is to become useless; to seek justification by the law is to fall away from grace. Seeking justification by law excludes grace; grace excludes law. The doctrinal point of Chapters 3-4 was that justification is by Christ only, without any additional requirements. This point is repeated here for emphasis as Paul begins to set forth the practical applications of the principle.

5:5-6. Paul, anticipating the hope of justification by faith, foreshadows the role of the Spirit. These verses prepare the way for Paul's extended explanation in vv. 16-26 of how walking by the Spirit enables Christian freedom and avoids license and ungodliness. In Christ Jesus, faith works by love and excludes the necessity of measuring Christianity by the outward standards that were being required by the Judaizers. The phrase "faith through love working" presents two possible understandings. Does "working" belong with faith or with love? In the context of Galatians and considering Paul's purpose in this section, faith is primary: faith works through love. The other option is less probable in the context: if love is considered primary in the context, the meaning is that faith is seen "through love working."

5:7-12. The singular pronoun is most likely stylistic, or it may be a collective singular. Paul is combatting the teaching of the false teachers. The Galatians were doing well, but now they have been hindered (*anakopto*, "cut off" continues Paul's use of metaphors related to a race) from obeying (*peitho*, being persuaded by, not the more common word for obedience) the truth. The idea that they have been persuaded by something other than the truth leads into v. 8. The persuasion they are experiencing is not from God (1:6). The proverb of v. 9 underscores the danger of accepting a little false persuasion or a little false teaching. Therefore, v. 10 accentuates Paul's confidence that they will not accept the different ideas that are being advanced by the false teachers. If the Galatians reject the false teachings, judgment will fall on those who are troubling them.

5:11-12. These verses are difficult to understand because we do not know all that was occurring. The Galatians understood Paul's point better than we do. "If I yet preach circumcision": apparently, the false teachers were accusing Paul of preaching circumcision. That is, in Paul's absence they were saying that Paul was actually in agreement with them. In the historical context, this accusation of the false teachers could refer to the circumcision of Timothy (Acts 16:3). Timothy was from Galatia (assuming the south Galatian theory, see the Introduction). The accusation was not true, as was obvious by the fact that Paul was being persecuted and opposed by the false teachers. In the context, the message of v. 11 should be understood thus: "to preach circumcision is to deny the need for the cross, and thus to remove the offense of the cross."

5:12. In v. 12, Paul uses hyperbole (exaggeration, not to be understood literally), an exaggeration that in essence says, "If a little cutting—circumcision—is good, why not do a little more cutting." The Greek literally says, "I wish also those troubling you would cut themselves off." The word for "cut themselves" is often translated as castration or emasculation. An alternative interpretation is that cutting refers to the false teachers being separated from or cut off from the Galatians, although the first option seems to fit the context best.

5:13-15. These three verses conclude the argument; Paul restates the major teaching of the passage (cf. 5:1). As was stated in the overview of the chapter, these last verses deal with the problem of turning freedom into license. Christian freedom is not an opportunity for indulgence; it is rather an opportunity for loving service one to another. Against the teaching of the Judaizers about the necessity of circumcision in order to keep the law, Paul cites Lev. 19:18 to show that love is the summary or fulfillment of the law (v. 14). Paul describes the impact of the false teachers on the Galatian churches, using the illustration of animals devouring each other. The ultimate result of letting such false teaching continue will be destruction.

5:16-26. The first verse of this paragraph continues the thought of vv. 13-15. Paul says that the way to avoid indulgence and fleshly desires is to walk in the Spirit. "To walk" is used figuratively for "to live." Christians are to live a life controlled by the Spirit. The use of the double negative is not reflected in most translations. Literally, "walk in the Spirit and the lust of the flesh 'by no means' you will complete" (carry out, fulfill, gratify). Paul emphasizes the utter impossibility of doing both simultaneously. The flesh and the Spirit are opposites. The contrast is apparent. The Christian walking in the Spirit will not (by no means) be involved in the sinful actions of the flesh.

     5:17. A literal translation helps clarify the last phrase in v. 17: "For the flesh lusts against the Spirit and the Spirit against the flesh, for these things oppose each other, lest you do whatever you want." Paul's point is that the opposition of these two forces—flesh and spirit—is what makes it possible for the Christian to avoid certain desires. The Christian does not do whatever she or he wants. The last phrase of v. 17 is parallel to the last phrase of v. 16. Paul's point is not lack of control—his point is exactly the opposite! Paul says that by walking in (by) the Spirit one can control fleshly desires. These verses provide a helpful commentary on Romans 7 where the text is often misunderstood to say that the Christian cannot control desires or actions. In Gal. 5:16-17 Paul says exactly the opposite! The Christian walking in the Spirit can control desires and actions; the law can never control desire. Galatians 5 and Romans 7-8 are in total agreement.

5:18. Walking by the Spirit frees one from being "under the law" (v. 18). Those who walk by the Spirit are not subject to the law and should not subject themselves to the law. The reference is to the Old Testament law, but by extension the principle applies to any legal system.

5:19-21. Paul continues the contrast with a list of the works of the flesh (vv. 19-21) and a list of the fruit of the Spirit (vv. 22-23). The list of the works of the flesh is somewhat longer than the list of the fruit of the Spirit (fifteen items vs. nine items). The list of the works of the flesh has been analyzed, categorized, and summarized in various ways. Since good descriptions of these concepts are available in other Bible study resources, they are not described in detail here. Of interest as one thinks of modern applications is the inclusion of "lesser sins" in the list: enmities, hatred, strivings, and jealousy, outbursts of anger, selfishness, rivalry, dissensions (disagreements, arguments), factions and envy. The sins in the list are not distinguished so that some are more important and others are less important—all are described as works of the flesh. The phrase, "things like these," indicates that other sins could be included. Those who practice such sins will not inherit God's kingdom.

5:22-23. In contrast with the list of the works of the flesh, Paul describes aspects of the Christian life which are fruit of (produced by) the Spirit. Some have suggested that Paul purposefully uses the word "fruit" to avoid confusion with the word "gifts." The idea probably comes more from analyzing the current state of Christianity than from reading the text of Galatians in its context. The characteristics listed in these verses flow naturally from the presence of God's Spirit within the believer. Again, there are good descriptions of these characteristics in other Bible study resources so they are not described in detail here. "Against such things there is no law" (v. 23).

5:24-26. The ones who are "of Christ" have crucified the flesh (cf. 2:20) with its passions (*pathema*, emotions, influences) and lusts (*epithumia*, desires). In the next phrase, Paul uses two different Greek words—to live (*zao*) and to walk (*stoicheo*, march in military order, keep in step, conform, walk orderly). If we live by the Spirit, let us also walk in step with the Spirit (v. 25). To walk by the Spirit is to behave in accordance with the Spirit, showing the fruit of the Spirit. These last verses of the chapter summarize the paragraph (vv. 16-26) but also serve as a summary of the chapter. Verse 26 echoes the thoughts of v. 15, again highlighting the disastrous consequences of the teaching being advanced by the false teachers. Let us not be vainglorious (conceited, haughty), challenging (*prokaleomai,* irritating, provoking) one another, and envying (*phthoneo*) one another.

Galatians 6

[Note: it is suggested that the introductory materials in this guide be reviewed before beginning your own preparatory reading and analysis.]

CONTENT

The paragraphing included in the Content section of each chapter gives suggestions and a possible guide. The student is encouraged to identify the paragraphs and subsections within each paragraph as part of his or her own reading, analysis, and study. In modern versions, there is general agreement about the division of this chapter into paragraphs.

<u>Outline of the Chapter</u>
6:1-10   The love and service of Christian liberty motivate the shared life
6:11-18   Final admonitions and postscript

<u>Observations about and Summary of the Contents of the Chapter</u>
Here is what life in the Spirit looks like. When others are caught in sin, spiritual people can carefully restore them, avoiding the temptation to share in the same negative attitudes or sins. Spiritual people willingly help carry the burdens of others. Such actions define what it means to love your neighbor, a principle that guides those whose allegiance is to Christ. Spiritual people avoid conceit and egotism—these are forms of self-deception. Each person knows how to evaluate himself before God without resorting to comparisons with others—which almost always has the purpose of building oneself up while tearing others down. All Christians should take care of their own responsibilities and challenges, but this does not mean that we are not willing to bless others when they are a blessing to us, or to help others even as we ourselves sometimes need help.

God understands and takes everything into account. If we are self-deceived, God is not deceived. We reap what we sow, whether of life in the Spirit or of life focused in the sinful things of the world. The purpose of this instruction is encouragement so that we will keep going, knowing that the reward is certain with God. This motivates us, especially when it comes to help- ing those who are part of God's family.

Here is the conclusion. What is impressive in the Chris- tian life is not visible externally. In fact, life in Christ is not about circumcision, obedience to legal demands, and boasting about such things. The only cause for boasting in Christ is that the cross of Christ has made possible my crucifixion to the world; even more, the world no longer has any interest in me or for me. What counts is that we are new creation in Christ and that the true Israel of God knows peace and the meaning of mercy.

STUDY HELPS
6:1-10. "Brothers" is a typical transition and often introduces a new topic. This chapter continues the practical section of Gala- tians (Chapters 5-6). Paul describes several actions that flow from a correct understanding of his gospel—love, service, rela- tionships, caring, and life in the Spirit.

6:1. If a fellow-Christian (*anthropos*, a man, used in a general sense, applying to both males and females) is discovered in a trespass (*paraptoma*, literally, a slip to the side; the word is a general description of sin that in this context refers to any kind of wrongdoing), spiritual persons are to restore such a person. Literally the text says, "If one is overtaken" (surprised), but the context indicates that other Christians are aware of the wrongdo- ing. Restoration is to be accomplished in a spirit of meekness, taking careful notice of oneself to avoid temptation. The temp- tation could be to participate in the same sins; more likely the temptation is to pride, being judgmental, and failing to forgive.

6:2. To carry one another's burdens fulfills the law of Christ (compare 1 Cor. 9:21). Two different words are translated burden or load in v. 2 (*baros*) and v. 5 (*phortion*). The word in v. 2 is the very heavy burden of a pack animal. The word in v. 5 is used of a soldier's pack.

6:3-5. These verses have to do with properly assessing oneself. "If anyone thinks (himself or herself) to be something while in fact being nothing (v. 3), such is self-deceiving." A proper self-understanding will smooth interpersonal relationships.

Christian relationships are a major theme in vv. 1-10. Each must test or prove his own work (v. 4) so that he will have reason for boasting in himself and not in comparing himself to another. In v. 5, each must bear (*bastazo*, same verb as v. 2) his own burden (the words used to describe the burdens in v. 2 and v. 5 are different; see comment on 6:2). The point is that each one must carry personal responsibilities, not depending on others to do what one should be doing for oneself.

    6:6-10. These verses continue the theme of personal responsibility and healthy interpersonal actions from the previous verses. Those who receive teaching in the word should share with the teacher. "In all good (things)" is ambiguous; the exact nature of the "good things" to be shared is not explained in the text. The warning against deception is literally "do not be led astray" (*planao*, to wander about). We get our word planet from this Greek word that means wanderer. The specific point of the deception is likely described in what immediately follows. "Do not be deceived—God will not be ridiculed or made fun of." Therefore, each will receive according to what he sows— whether of flesh or Spirit (v. 8). The Spirit is the source of eternal life. The contrast of flesh and Spirit was introduced in 5:16-17. Do not lose heart (*ekkakeo*, to be weak or faint, to fail, to be weary, to be discouraged) in doing good, because we will reap at the right time if we do not quit (*ekluo*, relax, fail, give up). Opportunity in v. 10 is "as we have time" (compare to 5:13, "as advantage"). The admonition of v. 10 repeats the phrase "the good"—let us do good to all but most of all to those of the household of faith.

6:11-16. The personal note of v. 11 likely shows that Paul is writing these words with his own hand, perhaps to verify the authenticity of the letter (cf. "I Paul" in 5:2). The idea of writing in large letters has been cited as possible support for problems with his eyesight.

    6.12. In vv. 12-16 is a summary of the letter. Those who want to look good outwardly are demanding circumcision. Paul suggests that the false teachers are concerned about outward signs of religion in order to avoid persecution. The meaning seems to be that by demanding that the Gentile believers be circumcised, they would avoid being castigated and rejected by Jewish brothers who had not accepted the message of the cross.

6:13. How is it possible that by simply demanding circumcision for Gentile believers the Jewish Christians could avoid being rejected by non-Christian Jews? If this is the question, Paul's response makes sense. Because those who are circumcised (Jews, whether unbelieving Jews or Jewish Christians) do not and cannot keep the law, they do not demand that all Jews keep every aspect of the law. The false teachers are only interested in circumcision so that they can boast about keeping the law with regard to the outward ritual. No one can successfully keep the entire law.

6:14-16. Paul's boasting and dependence is only in the cross. In the cross Paul has experienced crucifixion to the world (cf. 2:20). He has died to the world and the world has died to him. In the word "world" (*kosmos*) Paul is referring to concern for fleshly, temporal things. After death (described in v. 14) comes new creation. When one understands new creation in Christ, circumcision and uncircumcision are nothing. Understanding what God does in Christ makes the whole question about which the false teachers were so adamant a non-issue. Those who understand and live by this rule (*canon*, measuring stick), are in fact the Israel of God, the true people of God, sons and heirs.

6:17-18. Paul wishes for an end to the trouble he is experiencing for preaching a gospel that includes the Gentiles. He has suffered physically; his stoning in Acts 14 is one possible example. The lack of personal references in this letter may be explained by the fact that it is addressed to multiple churches. The final greeting is much like those in Paul's other letters.

Introduction to the Thessalonian Correspondence

A Quick Overview

- The Thessalonian letters are two of the earliest of Paul's letters and are among the earliest New Testament documents.
- The Thessalonian letters give insight into the work of Paul as a church planter and missionary. The letters reflect his concern for an infant church, a church that he had recently worked to establish.
- The letters reveal both the kind of church Paul wanted to establish and the problems which the new Christians encountered.
- The Thessalonian church is in many ways a model church.
- These letters describe the early proclamation of the gospel and the understandings and actions that resulted.

Background

Paul's arrival and stay in Thessalonica is recorded in Acts 17. The city was a port at the head of the Thermaic Gulf and was also on the Via Ignatia, a major Roman road. Thessalonica was the largest city in Macedonia, with a population of perhaps 200,000, and was an important center of commerce and politics. The name of the modern city today is Salonika. Thessalonica attracted people from various parts of the first-century world and was characterized by pagan religions and cultures. It has been estimated that as much as one-third of the population was Jewish in the first century.

Paul came to Thessalonica from Philippi where he had been imprisoned. Had his reputation preceded him to Thessalonica? The Bible does not give us an answer but it is certainly possible. Paul's custom was to begin his preaching in the synagogue. Because Philippi did not have a synagogue, Paul had preached outside the city by the side of the river. Thessalonica, however, did have a synagogue. Paul was accompanied by Silas (also known as Silvanus) and Timothy. Both are mentioned in the salutations of the letters Paul wrote to the Thessalonian church. Luke did not accompany the missionary group to Thessalonica but stayed at Philippi (based on the "we" passages in Acts).

Paul preached in the synagogue three Sabbaths. Four verbs are used in Acts 17 to describe his preaching: discussing, declaring, explaining, and saying. His message was that "Jesus is the Messiah." Those who responded favorably to his preaching included some Jews, some God-fearing Gentiles, and some noble women. The God-fearing Gentiles were familiar with Judaism and were often receptive to the gospel.

We do not know how long Paul was in Thessalonica on this first visit. He was there at least three weeks. In 1 Thessalonians 2 he speaks of working to support himself (his trade was tent-making). Philippians 4:16 says that the recently established Philippian church sent monetary gifts at least twice during his initial stay in Thessalonica. It is likely that he was in Thessalonica at least a month, possibly two to three months, before intense opposition arose from the Jewish leaders. As a result of the uprising and difficulty, Paul left the city by night and went to Berea. Based on references within the letters, it appears that the young church in Thessalonica continued to face intense opposition after Paul's departure.

Author and Date

Paul is the author; Timothy and Silas are also included in the salutations. Critics have questioned Paul's authorship of 2 Thessalonians but there is no solid evidence to contradict Pauline authorship. Some have hypothesized that the second letter preceded the first, but that theory is not widely accepted. Among the reasons given for maintaining the current order are (1) the apparent intensification of the problems in 2 Thessalonians, (2) possible references in 2 Thessalonians to a previous letter from Paul (2:2, 15; 3:17), and (3) the tone of the second letter, which better fits as a follow-up letter rather than as the initial letter.

The date of the letters is one of the more certain dates we can establish in the New Testament, based on the textual reference that Paul was brought before Gallio during his time in Corinth (Acts 18). Gallio served for a relatively short time in AD 51-52. Paul was in Corinth 18 months so there is some room for flexibility, but one can date the Thessalonian correspondence about AD 51-52 with some certainty. Working through the dates chronologically beginning with the Jerusalem Council (Acts 15) in AD 50, we read of Paul's departure from Antioch on the second journey, briefly passing by the previously established churches, traveling across Asia Minor, receiving the Macedonian call, and spending a brief time in Philippi before arriving in Thessalonica. This historical sequence yields a date of AD 50-51 for Paul's visit to Thessalonica, with the letters following closely thereafter.

Here is a timeline for Paul's letters, including approximate dates (AD), locations, and relationship to the book of Acts.

Date	Location	Bible Text	Letters Written by Paul
50	Jerusalem assembly	Acts 15	Gal written around this date
51-52	Paul in Corinth 18 months	Acts 18	1-2 Thess written around this date
53-56	Paul in Ephesus 3 years	Acts 19	1-2 Cor, Rom written during this time
	Overland trip	Acts 19-20	
58-60	In Jerusalem and Caesarea	Acts 21-26	("a little over 2 years")
60-62	First Roman Imprisonment	Acts 27-28	wrote Eph, Phil, Col, Philm
63-66	Additional travels	after Acts	wrote 1 Timothy, Titus
66-68	Last imprisonment	after Acts	wrote 2 Timothy

Reconstructing the Historical Timeline

After the meeting in Jerusalem (Acts 15, AD 50), Paul quickly visited the churches he had established on the first journey. Timothy joined the missionary group in Lystra (Acts 16). Paul then traveled westward across Asia Minor where he faced uncertainty as to which direction he should go. Receiving the "Macedonian call," he and his traveling companions went through Troas to Philippi (Acts 16) and afterward came to

Thessalonica (Acts 17:1). It appears that Luke stayed in Philippi, based on the "we" sections of Acts.

When problems arose in Thessalonica, Paul left that city for Berea (Acts 17), but problems also arose in Berea when some of the Jews from Thessalonica arrived. Paul left Berea for Athens, traveling alone. He instructed Silas and Timothy to join him as soon as possible. In Athens, he encountered philosophers and had little success, based on the narrative of Acts 17. Paul preached in Athens and then moved on to Corinth. At Corinth, Timothy and Silas joined Paul (Acts 18:5).

Based on the content of the first letter to the Thessalonians, Paul knew that he had left the infant church at a difficult and crucial time. At some point not long after his departure from Thessalonica, Paul sent Timothy back to Macedonia. Timothy spent time in Thessalonica, perhaps as long as six months (a longer period of time does not fit very well into the above timeline for the date of the book). When Timothy returned to Paul at Corinth, he brought positive news concerning the church in Thessalonica (1 Thessalonians 3). It was Timothy's report that led Paul to write the first letter to Thessalonica from Corinth. Paul addressed various questions and concerns, matters likely communicated by Timothy in his report.

It is generally thought that the second letter was written not long after the first when Paul became aware of additional problems facing the Thessalonian church. It seems likely that the second letter was written within six months of the first. As mentioned previously, some studies have suggested that the second letter was written before the first, but that view is not widely accepted.

Purpose of the Letters

By surveying the content of the first letter, we can say that Paul wanted

- To encourage the church toward faithfulness in the midst of persecution
- To address some criticisms that had been raised (perhaps by the Jewish opposition) concerning his motives

- To communicate the depth of his love and concern, along with his pride and his confidence in the new Christians
- To answer some specific questions, one of which concerned the return of Jesus

The contents of the second letter reflect some of the same concerns. Paul wanted
- To encourage the church in the midst of tribulations
- To correct possible misunderstandings about the Day of the Lord (the return of Jesus)
- To give instructions concerning some who had stopped working

A Few Other Matters

In this study of the Thessalonian correspondence, a summary of the message of the chapter is included with the outline, overview and observations at the beginning of the chapter. No footnotes are included in these Bible Study Guides since the content is considered general knowledge. No bibliography is supplied as I have worked primarily from the biblical text and from my own notes. At about the same time that I began working on this series, developing the various design and formatting elements, and preparing my study notes, I had the opportunity to review some online materials from Bob Utley. That I was favorably impressed is apparent in some of my explanations in this guide. At times, these notes build upon his treatment of the biblical text.

1 Thessalonians 1

[Note: it is suggested that the introductory materials in this guide be reread before beginning your own preparatory reading and analysis, especially for those who are not familiar with the five-step Bible study process.]

CONTENT

The paragraphing included in the Content section of each chapter merely serves as a suggestion or guide. The student is encouraged to identify the main paragraphs and subsections within each paragraph to assist in the development of his or her own study skills.

Outline of the Chapter

1:1	Greeting or salutation	
1:2-10	Thanksgiving for the Thessalonians' example	
	2-3	Thanksgiving
	4-10	Commendations

Observations about the Contents of the Chapter

After the customary salutation, Paul begins the book by saying how grateful he is for the rapid development of the Thessalonian church, especially in view of the circumstances that had whisked him and the original missionaries away from the city almost immediately. He prayerfully thanks God for their progress. That progress is evidence that they are convicted concerning the gospel, its power, and the role of the Holy Spirit. Anticipating the need to say something about the opposition that had arisen against him, Paul reminds them that he first came to Thessalonica with a message that helped both him and them to endure suffering.

Paul is encouraged, not only by how they received the message, but also because they shared it widely. The way in which Thessalonians had turned from idolatry to serve God and to live in hope was a model for other believers all across the region.

Overview: Summary of the Message

"Greetings! We are constantly grateful for you when we think about how you have responded to the gospel with faith, love, and hope. God chose you, and the gospel came to you powerfully in the Holy Spirit. You changed completed and became an example to all of the believers in Macedonia and Achaia. Everyone is talking about what happened at Thessalonica: how you changed completely and left idols and vain worship, that you now serve God wholeheartedly, and that you live in anticipation of Jesus' return. And with good cause! His resurrection declares our deliverance."

STUDY HELPS

1:1. Paul, Silas, and Timothy are mentioned as authors, although Paul is obviously the primary author. Silas and Timothy were with him when he wrote. They had also been with him during the establishment of the church. This verse reflects a standard greeting in the Greek epistolary form. Of interest is that Paul does not describe himself with a term of authority—such as "apostle"—even though he finds it necessary to defend his motives in Chapter 2.

The Thessalonians are described as a church (*ekklesia*). The Greek word as it was used in the first century referred to any kind of assembly.

1:2-10. These verses are part of one long prayer of thanksgiving that Paul offers on behalf of the Thessalonians. The admonition to "pray without ceasing" in 5:17 is well-known; more than once in the letter Paul mentions his unceasing prayer for the church. The section in 1:2-5 is one sentence that summarizes Paul's arrival, early ministry, and evangelism among them. This sentence includes a reference to each person in the Godhead.

1:3. Worthy of note is the mention of faith, love, and hope together. The relationship of the words in these phrases says that work is the result of faith, labor is the result of love, and perseverance is the result of hope. Timothy's report concerning the state of the church in Thessalonica probably included details about the spiritual progress of the Thessalonians. This was one of the reasons for Paul's thanksgiving to God.

1:4. Paul encourages the Thessalonians to recognize that they are loved by God and chosen by God.

1:5. The work, labor, and perseverance described in v. 3 are the result of the preaching of the gospel. Verse 5 begins with "because"—because our gospel did not come to you in word only, but in power, and the Holy Spirit, and full assurance. The gospel was preached; the gospel was visible in the example of the missionaries, an example that openly demonstrated the nature of their ministry and proved their commitment to the new believers while they were among the Thessalonians. The Thessalonians had responded to the gospel, and the gospel had changed their lives.

1:6-9. These verses describe the way the Thessalonians responded to the gospel. They became imitators of the Lord and of the missionaries, so that the Thessalonians themselves became examples. They were examples because of how they had received the message despite tribulation and opposition. They received the message with the joy that comes from the Holy Spirit. The news about how the gospel had entered Thessalonica and the response of these new believers spread (*execheomai*, literally, echo out) into all of Macedonia and Achaia, and in every place.

1:9-10. These verses describe the response of the Thessalonians to the gospel—past, present, and future. They turned to God from idols. This phrase may suggest that Paul in Thessalonica had a work among the Gentiles that extended beyond his previously-mentioned work with the God-fearers, since the God-fearers would have already rejected idolatry. "Idols" may be a figurative reference but there is no evidence to support that idea. It is also possible that Paul's description of the lives of the Thessalonian believers looked back further than their most recent conversion to Christ. Formerly, they had been idol-worshipers. They had turned from pagan practices and culture.

They had turned (*epistrepho*, past tense) to God to serve (*douleuo*, to serve as a slave, present tense) the living and true God, and to wait (present infinitive, reflecting future expectation) for his return. Paul concludes with a brief summary of the gospel: Jesus was raised from the dead by God, Jesus rescues us from coming wrath, Jesus will return from heaven to claim us.

References to Jesus' Return Occur
at the End of Every Chapter in 1 Thessalonians

1Thess. 1:10, and to wait for his Son from heaven, whom he raised from the dead, Jesus who delivers us from the wrath to come.

1Thess. 2:19-20, For what is our hope or joy or crown of boasting before our Lord Jesus at his coming? Is it not you? For you are our glory and joy.

1Thess. 3:13, so that he may establish your hearts blameless in holiness before our God and Father, at the coming of our Lord Jesus with all his saints.

1Thess. 4:16-17, For the Lord himself will descend from heaven with a cry of command, with the voice of an archangel, and with the sound of the trumpet of God. And the dead in Christ will rise first. Then we who are alive, who are left, will be caught up together with them in the clouds to meet the Lord in the air, and so we will always be with the Lord.

1Thess. 5:23, Now may the God of peace himself sanctify you completely, and may your whole spirit and soul and body be kept blameless at the coming of our Lord Jesus Christ.

An interesting characteristic of the book of 1 Thessalonians is that a reference to Jesus' return appears at the end of every chapter in the letter (see insert immediately above).

1 Thessalonians 2

[Note: it is suggested that the introductory materials concerning para-graphing (at the beginning of this guide) be read before beginning your own preparatory reading and analysis.]

CONTENT
The paragraphing included in the Content section of each chapter is only a suggestion. The student is encouraged to identify the paragraphs and subsections within each paragraph to assist in personal study. The paragraphing given here reflects most modern translations. Some translations divide vv. 1-13 into two separate paragraphs, vv. 1-6 and vv. 7-13. The Study Helps below use that division.

Outline of the Chapter
2:1-13   Paul's ministry in Thessalonica—motives and methods
2:14-16 The faith and patience of the Thessalonians in their current situation
2:17-20 Paul's desire to see the Thessalonians again

Overview of the Chapter
This chapter reflects the Jewish opposition that the Thessalonians were encountering and deals with various questions that had been raised about Paul's motives. It also outlines the attitudes, characteristics, and actions of an effective minister or missionary.

Overview: Summary of the Message
"You know that the time we spent with you produced great results. Even after what happened to us in Philippi, we came to you determined to take the gospel to new places, but we soon faced new opposition. The opponents accused us of ulterior motives, but you know that our hearts were pure, the message was true, and we were not trying to trick anyone. We wanted

only to declare the gospel that God gave us; there was no place for smooth words or greed.

"We were gentle, undemanding, and caring as we shared the gospel. We worked hard so we did not need any support from you. We lived right and shared a lot of fatherly advice, wisdom, and love as we encouraged you to live out the message of God. You recognized that it was God's message, and that it was not a human message.

"Now you are also suffering opposition. You are experiencing the same things God's people have suffered in the churches—the same kind of suffering that led to the death of Jesus and the deaths of the prophets before him. The Jews are against everyone, especially Gentiles! Will they ever get tired of doing wrong?

"After we were separated from you, we wanted to come to see you again and again, but Satan kept getting in the way. Nonetheless, you are our glory and joy when we think about Jesus coming again."

Observations about the Contents of the Chapter

Paul reminds the Thessalonians of how his ministry among them began. The fruits of his labor and the success of the gospel were immediately visible. He had had problems in Philippi before he came to Thessalonica. When problems arose in Thessalonica, those problems did not slow down the preaching of the gospel at all. In fact, had Paul and those with him had impure motives, the persecution would have been sufficient reason to simply move on. Paul endured the problems along with the Thessalonians because he had such a strong sense of having been entrusted with the gospel. His intention never was to please people; it always was to please God.

As an apostle of Christ, Paul would have been justified in asking for assistance with his living expenses while he was preaching, but he did not do that. He worked to earn his living and preached the gospel to the Thessalonians without burdening them. He dealt with them lovingly and kindly—encouraging, comforting, and exhorting them.

As he recounts this history of his time among them, Paul is grateful for the way the Thessalonians had received the gospel as the word of God in the midst of persecutions. The presence of persecutions means that they have had the same experience as countless Christian believers before them, suffering many things at the hands of the Jews who oppose the gospel. The opposition of the Jews is nothing new—the Jews also killed Jesus, and they killed the prophets before Jesus. A primary motivation of the Jews was to keep the gospel away from the Gentiles.

Paul would have liked to visit the Thessalonians, but he had not been able to do that. Nonetheless, he was proud of them; they were his glory and joy.

STUDY HELPS

2:1. "You know" is a phrase that occurs frequently in the book in slightly varying forms (1:4, 5; 2:1, 5, 10, 11; 3:3, 4; 4:3; and 4:13, that "you not be unknowing"). Similar phrases are "you remember" and "you do not need us to write." Paul uses the direct address multiple times in the book, "brothers."

2:1-6. I have made a division between the two subparagraphs at v. 6, based on the adversative conjunction "but" that introduces v. 7. In this first section (2:1-6), Paul explains his motives, methods, and ministry as he came among them. His arrival in Thessalonica was not in vain (for nothing, a failure). Even though the missionaries had suffered and been mistreated in Philippi (Acts 16), they remained bold to speak the gospel in Thessalonica where they also suffered much opposition. "Gospel of God" is likely a subjective genitive, the gospel that comes from God (see also vv. 8, 9) rather than the gospel about God.

2:3. The message of exhortation or encouragement did not come from error, from impurity (literally, from impure motives), or from deceit.

2:4. "To be approved by God" is literally "to be tested by God." That the missionaries had experienced and survived problems was proof of their authenticity. The missionaries were still being tested. They were entrusted with the gospel and spoke to please God, not to please human beings. That they were seeking to please God was a common way of explaining why there was opposition. The missionaries were shown to have pure motives because they withstood the examination by God.

2:5. With false or impure motives comes manipulation, but Paul had not come to Thessalonica with flattery or with greedy opportunism. Paul expands this point later in the chapter when he explains that he had worked at his trade to avoid being a burden to the Thessalonian church. He did not take money from them, although we know he did receive help from Philippi (Phil. 4:16). Paul's greatest supporting evidence for the sincerity of his ministry was that the testimony would be consistent even if God who knows all things were called as witness. This was a common way of declaring truthfulness.

2:6. Paul's use of the description "apostles" appears to include Timothy and Silas, illustrating that the word is used in the New Testament more broadly than in the sense of the Twelve. Examples include Barnabas (Acts 14:4, 14), Apollos (1 Cor. 4:6), James the Lord's brother (Gal. 1:19), and the group of church representatives responsible for the contribution for the poor saints in Jerusalem (2 Cor. 8:23). Literally, an "apostle" is "one who is sent." The broader use of the word "apostle" in the New Testament to describe some who were "sent" as messengers or representatives should be considered in interpreting 1 Cor. 12:28 and Eph. 4:11 where some were "gifted" to be apostles. Both of these passages appear to refer to persons other than the original twelve Apostles. This usage presents no problem when one understands the New Testament context and the varied use of the word. The question of whether the term "apostle" should be used to describe certain Christians today remains problematic, since the word is often misunderstood and its use tends to miscommunicate what is meant. Paul could have asserted his apostolic authority to make demands (possibly for financial compensation), but did not.

2:7-13. Paul continues a description of his ministry among the Thessalonians.

2:7. The varying translations of this verse in modern versions are due to a textual variant. Is the correct word infants (*nepios*) or gentle (*epios*)? The best reading is infants. We were as infants among you. Since the word *nepios* has roots that mean non-speaking, figuratively its use could mean something like, "We did not make many demands."

The message of the verse is little changed by the variants. The point is that Paul and his companions were gentle and non-demanding among the Thessalonians, in the same way that a mother (wet-nurse) nourishes her own children. For a similar use of the concept of infants, see the phrasing in 1 Cor. 14:20, "be infants with regard to malice."

2:8. The affection Paul felt for the Thessalonians was intense and deep—so deep that the missionaries not only were willing to share the gospel, they would have given their own lives to protect, nourish, and care for these new Christians. The missionary endeavor is empty and meaningless without such compassion and concern, and without the commitment and hard work reflected in the next verse.

2:9. You remember our hard work, how we toiled in manual labor. Paul's word usage in this statement suggests that he labored as a slave on behalf of the Thessalonian church. Paul often worked in his trade to support himself (1 Cor. 18), a practice that also served as an example to the Christians in the churches he established (cf. 2 Thess. 3:6-15). Rabbis were required to have a trade or method of livelihood. Paul says he worked day and night, likely referring to his work in tent-making by day and his work in preaching by night.

2:10. The truthfulness of what Paul was affirming was not in doubt. Not only was God a witness (v. 5), the Thessalonians were also witnesses. They had seen the behavior of the missionaries—holy, just and beyond reproach (devout, upright, and blameless).

2:11-12. Three verbs describe Paul's work: exhorting (*parakaleo*), encouraging (*parathumeomai*, consoling, comforting), and imploring (*martureo*, affirming, witnessing) that they walk in a way worthy of God, the One who calls us to share his kingdom and glory.

2:13. Paul again mentions his constant prayer of thanksgiving for the way the Thessalonians had received the Word of God (the gospel). They received it as God's word (a word coming from God), not as a human word. Paul says that the word is now at work in them. The verb form literally suggests that God's word is our energy—that it energizes those who receive it, accept it, and believe it.

2:14-16. The idea of imitation first appears in 1:6. In 2:14-16, the Thessalonians are imitators of Paul and the Judean churches in the matter of enduring suffering. "In Christ" is a common New Testament phrase, signifying union with Christ and participation in the body of Christ. The churches of the first century endured much persecution, both from the Romans and from religious people who rejected the exclusive nature of the gospel message. In this passage, the suffering is at the hands of the Jews who killed Jesus and the prophets, drove Paul out (possibly a reference to Acts 17:5-9), are not pleasing to God, and are hostile to all men so that they hinder Paul's speaking to the Gentiles so they can be saved. This reference may indicate that the influence of the Judaizing teachers had spread beyond the churches of Galatia. Also, this may reflect a more extensive work of Paul among the Gentiles in Thessalonica (that is, beyond his work with the God-fearers). Hostile to "all men" likely refers to the "nations," the Gentiles.

These actions of the Jews fill up the measure of their sins. The idea is that they are completing their evil deeds and that God's wrath comes on them.

2:17-20. Paul has previously used the figures of a mother and a father to describe his relationship with the Thessalonians. In the phrase "taken away" or "being separated" he uses a verb that means "to be orphaned" (*aporphanizo*). The word demands an agent or instrument (understood if not stated), so someone else (Jewish opponents?) was responsible for the separation. Paul's use of the word reinforces an important point because some were saying that his rapid departure and continuing absence showed his lack of concern and reflected impure motives. Paul affirms his care for the Thessalonians.

Paul greatly desired to see them, had wanted to come to them once and again, but was hindered by Satan. Paul considered the Thessalonian church to be an evidence of his apostleship and effective ministry. In the final verses of Chapter 2, Paul again mentions the coming of Jesus. At the coming of Jesus, the Thessalonians will be Paul's hope, joy, and crown, those in whom he will glory (take pride). "Glory" or "boasting" refers to Paul's joy and pride in serving God. This is not the glory that is to be attributed only to God. This verse should not be read in an exclusive sense so that the Thessalonian church will be Paul's glory, but that others he had taught will not.

"At his coming" (*parousia*) is literally "at his presence," but is metaphorically translated and understood as "coming," meaning not now present and at some time in the future present again. This is the first use of this Greek word in the book. The significance of the word is explained below in the Study Helps for Chapter 4.

1 Thessalonians 3

[Note: it is suggested that the introductory materials concerning paragraphing be reread before beginning your own preparatory reading and analysis. Those who are not familiar with the five steps of Bible study outlined in the introduction are encouraged to review those steps.]

CONTENT

The paragraphing and outline included in the Content section of each chapter give suggestions or guides. The division of the biblical text into paragraphs is fairly standard in modern translations, although the descriptive headings can vary significantly.

Reminder: the student is encouraged to read the text several times before beginning the detailed study, and to identify the paragraphs based on those readings. This occurs naturally when one follows the five steps outlined in the introduction.

Outline of the Chapter

3:1-5	Paul's concern for the Thessalonian church (continued from 2:17-20)
3:6-10	Paul's response to Timothy's good report
3:11-13	Paul's prayer concerning the Thessalonian church

Observations about the Contents of the Chapter

      The chapter division between Chapter 2 and Chapter 3 is somewhat artificial since 3:1-5 continues the thought that Paul began in 2:17-20. Chapter 3 is very personal; it concludes the first part of the book. Here is a brief paraphrase that catches the thrust of Paul's message to the Thessalonians (2:17-3:13):

> We wanted to come to see you but could not. I, Paul, especially wanted to come to see you. We want you to know that we are grateful for you and your progress. I kept wanting to come to see you, so we eventually decided that we should send Timothy to find out about you. We did not

want you to become discouraged by the opposition.

Now he has come back with a good report about you. How encouraged we are by that report! We are encouraged to go on because we know you are standing firm. We are grateful and we continue to pray for you so that we can come to see you, so you will grow in love, and you will be strong and ready for the day Jesus comes.

Overview: Summary of the Message of the Chapter

"Here's what happened. We were so concerned that we decided to send Timothy to find out about you and to encourage you. We all knew persecution was coming, and Satan's temptation is hard to overcome. When Timothy came back with a glowing report of your faith and love, and news of your affection for us, we were encouraged. Nothing helps us stand taller or feel more alive than receiving such good news! We are thankful for you, and we pray for you constantly so you will have all that you need.

"Our prayer is that God will bring us together again, and that you will always abound in love with a strong commitment to holiness until Jesus comes."

STUDY HELPS

3:1-5. Paul describes his deep concern for the Thessalonians and some of the background of the decision to send Timothy to verify the situation in the church in Thessalonica. The plural first person, "we," may be an "editorial we," or it may suggest that the team agreed together on the plan to send Timothy. In Acts 18:5, we learn that both Silas and Timothy had been in Macedonia and came to Paul in Corinth. It appears that Paul was alone in Athens (Acts 17). The Bible does not give more details concerning the travels and locations of Paul, Silas, and Timothy during this time. Paul's words as he describes the decision to send Timothy suggest that he had reached a "breaking point." He had no rest since he did not know how the Thessalonians were getting along. Here we see the heart of a missionary who is concerned about those he has taught. The word that is translated "to be left behind" may reflect another family or parental metaphor.

Paul's description of Timothy shows that Paul was sending someone that he considered his own representative, someone who was very capable in sharing and defending the gospel. The use of the word gospel in v. 2 has an interesting counterpoint later in this chapter. Paul's purpose in sending Timothy was to confirm (*sterizo*, strengthen, establish) the faith of the Thessalonians and to encourage (*parakaleo*, exhort, console) them, so that they would not be disturbed by the opposition they were enduring.

3:3-4. Paul reminds the Thessalonian church that persecution can be expected as part of God's plan, a concept he had applied to himself in 2:2, 15 and to the Thessalonians in 2:14. This was apparently something he had told them about repeatedly.

3:5. This verse serves as a summary with the added detail that Paul was fearful concerning their faith (faithfulness), afraid that Satan had tempted them to leave the faith and that the previous work in Thessalonica had been in vain (cf. 2:1).

3:6-10. The news that Timothy brought from Thessalonica is described as "good news," using the Greek word that is usually translated "gospel." This is the only use of this word in the New Testament to describe news other than the good news of the gospel. Timothy was indeed a laborer in good news (3:2), twice over!

The good news that Timothy brought from Thessalonica concerned the faith and love of the infant church, perhaps pointing back to 1:3. Love can be toward God or toward one another. Based on 3:12, the latter may be preferable. The Thessalonians were supporting and caring for one another. Paul also considered it good news that the Thessalonian church members wanted to see Paul just as Paul wanted to see them. This mutual desire shows that the relationship was firmly in place and that the accusations (of false motives and methods) that had been leveled against Paul by the opponents had not turned the church against Paul.

Just as the Thessalonians were experiencing affliction, Paul had also suffered rejection and difficulties in Athens and in Corinth. In the face of such afflictions, the word that Timothy brought was comforting (v. 7, another occurrence of the verb *parakaleo* in the same context).

3:8. "Now we are really alive" is a metaphorical way to express relief. Paul was relieved that the Thessalonians were standing firm; he was hoping that they would continue to stand firm.

3:9-10. A rhetorical question provides a segue to the prayer than concludes the chapter (a prayer that also serves to conclude the first part of the letter). "What thanksgiving can we return to God for you, for all the joy that we feel for your sake before our God, as we pray most earnestly night and day that we may see you face to face and supply what is lacking in your faith?" (ESV) Note the repeated reference to Paul's constant, persistent, earnest prayer for them.

The reference to what is lacking in faith may be a way to anticipate the question about the coming of Jesus, a question to which Paul will turn in the last part of Chapter 4 (4:13-18). The subjects Paul addresses in 4:1-12 could also be included in the phrase "what is lacking."

3:11-13. These verses are one sentence in Greek, with three verbs in the optative mood (direct, increase, abound). The optative mood is rare in the New Testament, but it is used here since it is the potential mood, common in prayers. Paul prays that God the Father will help clear the way for Paul's visit to them. For the Thessalonians, he prays for increasing and abounding love, for one another and for all people.

The goal of the prayer is that God will establish (*sterizo*) their hearts with a strong commitment so they will be blameless and holy at Jesus' coming. At the conclusion of the chapter, we again find a reference to the coming of Jesus. As noted earlier, that each chapter of the letter concludes with a reference to the return of Jesus is a characteristic of this letter.

1 Thessalonians 4

[Reminder: it is suggested that the student review the introductory materials about paragraphing before beginning preparatory reading and analysis. This is an important part of developing a useful Bible study process that will help develop the habits that lead to reading with understanding.]

CONTENT

The paragraphing and outline included in the Content section of each chapter are merely suggestions or guides. The student is encouraged to identify the paragraphs (and subsections within each paragraph) as part of her or his own study. In the principal modern translations, there is general agreement concerning the division of this chapter into paragraphs. Based on your own reading, and without consulting other sources, how would you describe the content of the paragraphs? What headings would you use?

Outline of the Chapter

4:1-8	Living a pure life pleasing to God (introductory remarks; sexual purity)
4:9-12	Living an orderly life
4:13-18	The coming of the Lord (continues in 5:1-11)

Observations about the Contents of the Chapter

Paul introduces the chapter with the word "finally." This word is transitional, but Paul may have had in mind that he was moving to the final subjects he wanted to address—the Christian lifestyle and questions about Jesus' return. These concerns may have been reported by Timothy. Paul's treatment of the theme of Jesus' return (4:13-18) will continue in 5:1-11. Here is a brief summary of the essence of the message of Chapter 4:

> What we have shared with you is how to live to please God. God wants holy lives, without immorality, passion, and lust. God wants us to live in love and quietness.

Now I want to clarify for you some details about Jesus' return, so you can live in hope without the kind of grief that characterizes those who live without hope in the future. Jesus will return and those who have died will be resurrected so we can all rise to meet Christ in the air. Share these words of encouragement.

Overview: Summary of the Message

This expanded summary of the message of the chapter incorporates the principle themes Paul uses.

"As I come to the end of this letter, remember the instructions about how God wants us to live. Because his will is for our sanctification, avoid immorality and live honorably. I do not need to remind you about brotherly love—you are doing that as you live and work peaceably.

"I want to write briefly about those who have died in Jesus so you will not grieve like people without hope. Because Jesus died and rose, we know that God is able to raise those who have died. He will bring them with him so we will not have any advantage or get out in front of them. When Jesus comes, they will be raised and we will quickly join them as we are taken up together, so we will all meet Jesus in the air to be with him forever. Everyone needs encouragement so share these words."

STUDY HELPS

4:1-8. "Finally," literally "as to the rest." In this context, the phrase suggests transition more than conclusion. We have previously noted Paul's repeated use of the term of address, "brothers." The use of words of direct address may be helpful in outlining the book as they often indicate the start a new subject. (Greek grammar has a vocative case that is used for direct address. The use of forms of address to subdivide the text is especially obvious and helpful in studying the book of James.)

4:1. The verbs "request" and "exhort" may soften these instructions which are repeated from Paul's teaching when he was with them—instructions they were well aware of. The overall subject is how they should walk (live) and (in order to) please God. ("To please God" is omitted in some later manuscripts, but it is included in this guide based on the evidence.) The specific subject is holiness or sanctification.

4:3-6. These verses are one sentence in Greek. God's will for Christians is holy lifestyles and character. Justification and sanctification should not be separated. A distinction between justification and sanctification is made in the doctrine of some religious groups. They limit sanctification by identifying it as God's work in the life of a Christian after salvation; that is, sanctification is something totally separate from salvation. In this passage, holy living is defined as follows: (1) to abstain (keep yourself) from fornication (all inappropriate sexual activity), (2) to know how to control (literally, acquire, take possession of) your own "vessel" in holiness and honor rather than in inordinate passion like the Gentiles, and (3) not to overreach and deceive your brother in this "matter" since the Lord will avenge all things. In v. 7, the call the purity and sanctification (holiness) is repeated.

What is the meaning of "vessel?" The two principal options are one's own body or one's wife. What is the "matter" under consideration? The two principal options are with regard to sexual conduct or with regard to business matters. Since the infinitive in v. 6 (*huperbaino*, overreach, go beyond, defraud, take advantage) has the article before it, it most likely refers back to vv. 3-5, connecting it to the context and the teaching about sanctification. In the context, it is not easy to justify a change of subject. The word that Paul uses is a word associated with business dealings, but it may serve as a euphemism here to soften the language. Finally, "brother" may relate to other believers or it could refer to humanity in general. My preference, as reflected in the comments below, is a reference to other believers.

4:7-8. These verses summarize the section (4:3-8). What is the message of this section? God's desire is holiness. Holiness must be part of one's overall conduct in the world (keeping oneself away from fornication), it must characterize the marital relationship, and it must be reflected in all relationships within the church, including how brotherly love (v. 9) is demonstrated in the church. There is no place for sexual liberties. Such liberties would abuse or take advantage of a brother who is responsible for the well-being of his household. (Seen in this light, the concept of going out of bounds, defrauding, or taking advantage of a brother makes sense.)

Paul had previously taught that the Lord avenges all such things with justice. Sanctification has always been the message of the gospel. Sanctification has always been God's will, as is reflected in God's calling. To reject this teaching is to reject God, and by extension to reject the Holy Spirit that God gives to the believer.

4:9-12. Paul now addresses the need for orderly living, especially with regard to interpersonal relationships. Brotherly love is not a new subject. The Thessalonian church does not need more written instructions; they have been taught this principle by God (through God's messengers) and they are practicing it toward one another and toward all the brothers in Macedonia. Nonetheless, it would be good to grow and excel in love.

The orderly life (vv. 11-12) includes living in tranquility, attending to your own business, working (a command Paul had previously given them; see also the example of Paul in 2:9), behaving properly toward non-Christians, and not needing others to rescue you. "Working with your hands" reminds of the example of Paul that was just cited, and also foreshadows Paul's instructions concerning those who quit working in anticipation of Christ's return (cf. 2 Thess. 2:1-4; 3:6-15). The instructions of vv. 11-12 give an interesting insight and alternative to the interpretation of v. 6 as set forth above. By failing to work and provide for oneself and one's family, relying on the brethren could be seen as taking advantage and defrauding in a financial matter. The word for defraud is related to greed.

4:13-18. This section extends into Chapter 5 (5:1-11), but in these study guides, the chapter divisions are used to outline the study insofar as possible.

Timothy had perhaps brought some questions from Thessalonica, or it may be that he had reported the lack of understanding and the doubts of some of the Thessalonians. Certainty concerning the truth gives stability to faith. Paul writes to inform them ("I do not want you to be uninformed") so that they will have hope and will not be sorrowful as many are at the death of loved ones. The primary motivating question for this section appears to be, "What will happen to believers who die before Jesus comes?" The early church, including Paul, believed in the imminent return of Jesus. In 2 Thessalonians 3:6-15 we learn that some had quit their jobs to wait for Jesus' coming. The Maranatha prayer was common in the church of the first century: "Come, Lord Jesus!" Christians were looking forward to seeing and participating in Jesus' return. But as time passed—in the case of the Thessalonians it had been only a brief time—life continued and loved ones died. What will happen to these? A second concern of Paul was that with the passing of time, anticipation waned and some Christians became lax concerning the Christian life. These two matters are good reasons to make certain we understand correctly the teachings of this section. These are important concerns for the contemporary church. What will happen when Jesus returns? How can we encourage Christians who have become lax in the Christian walk?

"Those who have fallen asleep" is a euphemistic way of referring to those who have died (Matt. 27:52; John 11:11-13; Acts 7:60; 1 Cor. 7:39, 11:30, 15:18; 2 Pet. 3:4). From the perspective of this world, it may appear that the dead are merely sleeping, but biblically we understand that they are alive, conscious, and awaiting the end of the world. Almost universally in my experience, Christians wish the Bible gave more details and clearer teaching about the state of the dead between death and the last resurrection day when both good and bad will be resurrected (John 5:28-29). Grieving at the death of a loved one may be normal as one thinks of separation and unfulfilled hopes and dreams. Paul does not say that Christians will not grieve, only that we will not grieve as others do. In the face of physical death, Christians have hope because of the gospel: Jesus died, Jesus was resurrected, God will bring with Jesus at his coming those who have died in him. The first class condition in v. 14 indicates that these truths are certain.

Paul's point is that since God had the power to resurrect Jesus from the dead, he has the same power for believers. (1 Corinthians 15 gives more detail about the resurrection, and says that resurrected Christians will have celestial bodies.) The text in 1 Thessalonians 4 affirms that Jesus is coming back to be joined with those Christians who are still living, and that those who have died are already with him. The phrase "will bring with him" troubles some. Since those who die are placed in tombs here on earth, our sense is that they are already here. The Bible says that their natural, physical bodies are in the natural, physical realm although decaying or decayed, but that they are in the spiritual realm. In this sense, they also will come (God will bring them) when Jesus comes, or in an alternative translation, God will also lead them away when Jesus comes. The Greek verb, *ago*, has semantic breadth that allows alternate translations (will bring, will lead, will lead away). In the context, the idea that God will also lead them away when Jesus returns may be better.

4:15-16. Paul speaks "by the word of the Lord." What Paul writes is not merely Paul's opinion. Those who are alive, that is, those who remain until the coming of the Lord, will not go ahead or have any advantage over those who have died. (The use of "we" may reflect Paul's expectation of the imminent return of Jesus, or it may be an "editorial we.")

The question Paul is addressing concerns believers, not unbelievers. This text does not say that unbelievers will not experience the same resurrection at the same time. This text says nothing about unbelievers. This text addresses only the situation of believers, apparently in answer to a question from the Thessalonians. Other Bible teaching makes clear that there will be one general resurrection of both the good and the bad ("the hour is coming") and that all will appear together before God (John 5:28-29).

Those who have died before Jesus' coming will fully participate in his coming. What will happen? The Lord will return personally, descending from heaven. Jesus promised that he would return (John 14:1-3). He will return with a commanding shout, an archangel's voice, and the sound of God's trumpet. The coming will not be secret (Rev. 1:7). No one will miss the command of the Lord. Trumpets functioned as announcements and as warnings. Trumpets are also mentioned in the context of resurrection in 1 Cor. 15:52.

4:17-18. Paul continues his answer to the question. At the coming of Jesus, those who have died in Christ (v. 14) will be resurrected first (before anything happens to the believers who remain). This terminology does not deny v. 14, the statement that "God will bring them or lead them." The first thing that will happen is that the bodies of those who have died in Christ will be resurrected (compare again, 1 Corinthians 15:35-57). Next, those who remain (are yet living) will be snatched up.

This verb, *harpazo*, which I have translated snatched up, is the word from which the concept of rapture comes. The Greek verb has limited use in the New Testament (Matt. 11:12, 12:29, 13:19; John 6:15, 10:12, 28, 29; Acts 8:39, 23:10; 2 Cor. 12:2, 4; Phil. 2:6; 1 Thess.4:17; Jude 23, Rev. 12:5.) The root has three basic meanings: (1) something done with much force, (2) something done for oneself or own benefit (see Phil. 2:6 for an example), and (3) something that occurs rapidly and unexpectedly. The context of 1 Thess. 4:17 suggests that the third meaning fits best in the context. The coming of Jesus will be sudden and unexpected.

Based on biblical teachings, it is hard to understand how the events described in these verses could occur in secret. Further, it is hard to understand how the unbelievers could be excluded. As noted earlier, in this passage Paul is not addressing the question of what will happen to unbelievers at Jesus' coming.

Believers will meet the Lord in the air and go with him to be with him forever. The text suggests that Jesus will not return to the earth. "Together" signifies both those who have died and those who remain alive. The early church had questions about the details of Jesus' return. The second letter will address additional questions. With this reference to the coming of Jesus at the end of Chapter 4, we see the pattern continued—a reference to the coming of Jesus appears at the end of every chapter in 1 Thessalonians. These were words of comfort for the Thessalonians.

This is perhaps not the place to address millennial questions since nothing is said of the 1000 years in the text. On the other hand, in most millennial theory, the rapture is a significant part of the theory, including teachings about a secret coming of Jesus and two separate resurrections. Sufficient to indicate that the subject is not as clear as some premillennialist teachers would have us think is this quotation from George Eldon Ladd, "I admit that the greatest difficulty to any premillennialism is the fact that most of the New Testament pictures the consummation as occurring at Jesus' *parousia.*" (While I have lost the exact source of the quote, the same conclusion is set forth in Ladd's *The Presence of the Future: The Eschatology of Biblical Realism.*) The connection between Jesus' coming and the end of the world is certainly clear to Paul in this text.

1 Thessalonians 5

[Note: it is suggested that the student reread the introductory materials about paragraphing before beginning to read, analyze, and study a new chapter of the biblical text.]

CONTENT
The paragraphing included in the Content section of each chapter is only a suggestion or guide. The student is encouraged to identify the paragraphs and the subsections within each paragraph to assist in his or her own study. The division of the biblical text into paragraphs is fairly standard in modern translations, although the content as described in the paragraph headings varies significantly.

Outline of the Chapter
5:1-11	The coming of the Lord (continued from 4:13-18)
5:12-22	Various exhortations (with 15 present imperatives)
5:23-24	Closing prayer
5:25-28	Salutation and blessing

Observations about the Chapter and a Summary of the Message
     In the first part of the chapter, Paul continues his explanation concerning details of Jesus' return. Some final instructions follow before the brief closing. This summary catches the message of the chapter:
     "Here is the rest of the story about Jesus' coming. I think you already know this and that we do not need to write to you about such things. Jesus' coming will be quick and sudden; it will be unexpected. Because we are children of the day, we walk in light and not in darkness. That means we walk in self-control, faith, and love, not in sinfulness and drunkenness. You know well what it means to walk in darkness. God has provided everything necessary for our salvation, whether we live or whether we die before Jesus returns.
     "Finally, consider those who labor as leaders among you. Encourage the weak, the timid, and those who not working. Live

out your faith, living in the Spirit, hold on to truth. And God will provide all you need."

STUDY HELPS

5:1-11. The continuation of Paul's discussion about the coming of Jesus helps correct misunderstandings and questions, especially with reference to what will happen to unbelievers when Jesus returns. "Brothers" marks the transition to a new section (but not a new topic in this case).

Since Paul does not need to say more about the times (*chronos*) and seasons *(kairos)* beyond what he has written in 4:13-18, this section should be understood as clarification or explanation. The "day of the Lord" is an Old Testament phrase that sometimes referred to a day of judgment and at other times to a day of blessing. In this text, it refers to a single day—a day of blessing on the faithful and judgment on the unbelievers. This day is the same day as was referenced in 1 Thess. 4:13-18, a day when all human beings will meet Jesus.

The day will come unexpectedly (a concept that is reflected in the Greek word *harpazo,* snatched up) in 4:17. (See discussion at 4:17 where the "unexpected" aspect of the word *harpazo* is explained.) The day will come at a most unexpected moment and destruction will be immediate. Note the contrast between the unbelievers (v. 3) and the believers (v. 4), referring to two groups experiencing the same event and the same day. This passage supports the idea of one general resurrection at the end of time. Paul describes the judgment as coming unexpectedly as do labor pains (also emphasizing suddenness) and as inescapable.

In comparison to the experience of the unbelievers on that day, believers do not have to be surprised by the events because Paul has taught them (1) what will occur, and (2) that they should remain ready. Paul describes the contrast in terms of light and darkness, day and night. "Sons of light" and "sons of day" (v. 5) are descriptions of the righteous; the idea of being "a son of" indicates those who share the nature of light and day. Let us not sleep (v. 6) is a different word than that used in 4:13-14. As Paul makes clear, the point of the admonition is "let us be alert and sober."

5:8-11. The believer is prepared for Jesus' coming by being equipped with the armor of faith, love and hope (compare 1:3). The result is salvation through the Lord Jesus Christ. The gospel is again summarized: "he died for us so that we might live with him, both those who have died and those who remain alive." The thought in v. 10 points back to 4:13-18. Verse 11 is parallel to 4:18—encourage and edify one another with these words, as you are doing.

5:12-22. "Brothers" indicates another transition. Apparently, the infant Thessalonian church had some kind of developed, organized leadership at this early stage. The discussion of the date of the letter (see Introduction) places the letter within a year or less of the first visit of the missionary team. The early establishment of leaders also characterized the churches established on the first missionary journey (Acts 14:21-23). The church is exhorted to recognize (respect) those who labor within the church (among you). The word for labor is more intensive than work. These leaders are "set before you" (literal translation) and they "put sense into you" (literal translation, often translated "admonish"). These are descriptions of those in charge (those who preside). That they are responsible for instructing and admonishing suggests spiritual wisdom. Concerning such leaders, have respect for them because of their work. The verbs used in these verses describe important aspects of biblical leadership.

In this passage (5:12-22) are fifteen imperatives that give instructions about how to live.
Live in peace.
Warn the idle (non-workers?).
Encourage the discouraged.
Help the weak.
Be patient with everyone.
Do not repay evil with evil.
Pursue what is good for one another and for everyone.
Rejoice always.
Pray without ceasing.
Give thanks in everything as is God's will, even in persecution.
Do not restrain the Spirit.
Do not treat prophecies with contempt, [but]

Examine everything (prove all things).
Hold on to what is good.
Abstain from every form of evil.

5:23-24. These verses are Paul's closing prayer. The salutation with which he began the letter included grace and peace. He closes with a reference to the God of peace. God is the one who sanctifies (4:1-8). The tripartite description of human beings as spirit, soul, and body is unique. Soul and spirit are often used as synonyms. There are fine shades of meaning in these words, especially in the Old Testament: body is the physical being, soul is the breath of life, and spirit is the eternal aspect. In the New Testament soul and spirit are often subsumed into the same concept. God not only sanctifies, he preserves. Paul's prayer is for the sanctification, preservation, and blamelessness of the Thessalonians at the Lord's coming. Note again the reference to the coming of Jesus at the end of this chapter. God is faithful to answer Paul's prayer and to do what Paul has asked.

5:25-28. The final section of the book includes both the closing salutation and a blessing.

5:25. As Paul has prayed for the Thessalonians, he requests their prayers also on his behalf. Such a request is common in Paul's letters (Eph. 6:18-19; Col. 4:3-4).

5:26-27. The holy kiss was a sign of love and community. The letter was to be read to the entire church. Paul's letters were intended for public reading.

5:28. In the final verse, Paul may have written by hand to authenticate the letter (compare 2 Thess. 3:17-18). As Paul began the letter mentioning grace and peace (1:1-2), so he ends the letter (5:23, 28).

2 Thessalonians 1

[Note: it is suggested that the introductory materials concerning paragraphing be read before beginning preparatory reading and analysis.]

CONTENT
The paragraphing included in the Content section of each chapter is intended only to provide suggestions or guides. The reader is encouraged to identify the paragraphs and subsections within each paragraph as part of his or her own study. In this chapter, modern translations are in general agreement concerning the division of the biblical text into paragraphs.

Outline of the Chapter
1:1-2 Greeting or salutation
           1:3-4, thanksgiving
           Note: these verses are sometimes outlined as a separate section, see comments below
1:3-12 Judgment at Christ's coming

Observations about the Contents of the Chapter
        The salutation is followed by a word of thanksgiving and a prayer. The first chapter is devoted to introductory matters typical of the Greek epistolary form. In preparation for the treatment of questions about the coming of Jesus (the day of the Lord) in Chapter 2, Paul makes several affirmations about Jesus' coming in Chapter 1. At Jesus' coming, God will punish those who reject Jesus and will reward those who have persevered. In this way, God will fulfill his purpose and reward faith.

Overview: Summary of the Message
        "Paul, with Silas and Timothy, grace and peace! We thank God because your faith is flourishing. Because of how you are persevering in the midst of persecutions, we are talking about you everywhere we go.

"You show that you yourselves are worthy when you show how good and just God is. God will right all injustices when Jesus is revealed. When Jesus comes, those who do not know God and have not obeyed the gospel will be destroyed, forever separated from God. What a glorious day that will be when Jesus' glory is declared. I am praying that you will also glorify him in your lives as your faith works out the goodness you long for."

STUDY HELPS

The letter of Second Thessalonians has as a primary purpose the development and explanation of the eschatological ideas that were introduced in 1 Thessalonians. Some people, not identified in the text, were suggesting that the events described by Paul, especially regarding the return of Jesus, had already occurred.

1:1-2. Paul, originally Saul and first called Paul in Acts 13:9, identifies himself without any additional description (such as apostle, servant, etc.). Silvanus (Silas) traveled with Paul on the second missionary journey (Acts 15:22-23, 40; 16:19-40) and was included in the salutation of the first letter. Timothy was also included in the salutation of the first letter. The salutation follows a pattern that is common in the Greek letter form: authors, recipients, greetings.

1:3-12. As indicated in the content outline above, some outlines identify the thanksgiving of vv. 3-4 as a separate section. I prefer to consider vv. 3-12 as a single paragraph since vv. 3-10 are one sentence in Greek. The last two verses of the chapter (vv. 11-12) serve a fitting summary of vv. 3-10.

1:3-4. Paul was thankful because of the growing faith and increasing love of the Christians in Thessalonica. Apparently, he had received additional news from them, including an update on their situation and an additional question or concern about the day of the Lord (2 Thess. 2:1-4). The Christian community in Thessalonica was being supportive of its members; Paul wished that their love would grow even more. The Thessalonian church was a source of pride for Paul and his coworkers (v. 4, compare also 1 Thess. 2:17-20). Paul specifically mentions their perseverance and faith in the midst of the persecutions and tribulations they were enduring.

1:5. The persecutions demonstrated God's just judgment. This statement is interesting when seen in the overall context. God will judge unbelievers justly. The Thessalonians have become believers and are now being judged unjustly (by their opponents), but they will one day receive God's just judgment, and as a result they will be counted worthy of the kingdom for which they are suffering. This is one of several New Testament passages where God's judgment is considered positive rather than negative for the believer. This verse shows Paul's understanding of the "already" nature of the kingdom in the first century, even though there is also a "not yet" element.

1:6-10. The first class conditional statement is assumed to be true. It is only right (just) that God will repay with tribulations those who are causing the Thessalonians to suffer tribulations. Paul included himself since he was also suffering. In this world, the Thessalonians and Paul were suffering tribulations, but when the Lord Jesus comes, they will have rest. The word used to describe this coming of Jesus is *apocalupsis* (revelation). The New Testament uses three words to describe the coming of Jesus: *parousia*, presence; *epiphania*, appearing; *apocalupsis*, revelation. These Greek words are not always translated into English consistently. In studying the return of Jesus, understanding which word is used is often significant. It is worth the effort to identify the original word.

The revelation (coming) of Jesus will be with mighty angels and flaming fire, indicating God's judgment. The judgment of God will come as retribution (vengeance, penalty) upon those who do not know God and do not obey the gospel of our Lord Jesus Christ. Because God can be known (that is, it is possible to know God), this phrase refers to willful rejection of the knowledge of God and willful rejection of God's will. Knowledge is not only cognitive, as in mental assent, but refers also to intimate relationship. There is no reason to identify two groups in v. 8, one without knowledge of God (Gentiles?) and another not obeying the gospel (Jews?), as some have suggested. All of those who fit the description will suffer the pain (penalty, from the same root as retribution in v. 8) of eternal destruction or separation from the presence of the Lord and from the glory of his power.

This judgment will occur when the Lord comes (*erchomai*) to be glorified by his saints. This can mean (1) that Jesus will receive glory from Christians, (2) that Jesus will be receive glory because the Christians have endured, or (3) that Jesus will be glorified in or among the Christians. In the New Testament, "saints" means "holy ones," a reference to those who are sanctified, thus Christians. When Jesus comes on that day (the same day as in 1 Thessalonians 4-5), he will be admired by all believers, including the Thessalonians who had believed the testimony of the missionaries.

1:11-12. Paul again mentions his constant prayer for the church, describing in more detail the content of his prayer. He is praying that God will count them worthy of the life he called them to live and that he will complete his purpose of goodness and every work of faith by his power. The result will be that the name of our Lord Jesus Christ will be glorified in them, and they in Him, according to grace.

2 Thessalonians 2

[Note: it is suggested that the introductory materials concerning para-graphing be read before beginning any preparatory reading and analysis of the chapter.]

CONTENT

The paragraphing included in the Content section of each chapter only serves as a suggestion or guide. The student is encouraged to identify the paragraphs, and subsections within each para-graph, to assist in his or her own study of the biblical text. A standard translation will be helpful in this task since the division of the biblical text into paragraphs is fairly standard in modern translations.

Outline of the Chapter

2:1-4	Questions about the coming of the Day of the Lord
2:5-12	Description of apostasy and lawlessness
2:13-17	Stand firm

Observations about the Contents of the Chapter

One of Paul's primary reasons for writing the second let-ter is to correct misunderstandings about some teachings that claimed the Lord had already returned, or that the day of the Lord had already come. Summarizing briefly, Paul affirms that the day has not yet come for two reasons: first, the apostasy has not yet occurred, and second, the true nature of lawlessness has not been made known or revealed. Paul explains all of this in detail in vv. 5-12. Since the day has not come, the admonition to the Thessalonians is "to stand firm."

Overview: Summary of the Message

For a summary of the message of this chapter, see the summary at 2:1-12 and the comments on the final five verses of the chapter.

Overview: Introduction to the Chapter

This chapter makes clear that the letter of 2 Thessalonians has as its primary purpose the development and explanation of the eschatological themes that were introduced in the letter of 1 Thessalonians.

Although this chapter seems complex, a careful study and analysis yields a basic understanding of Paul's message, even when every detail is not clear to the modern reader. The Thessalonians undoubtedly understood what Paul was saying because they were familiar with the teachings he mentions. Let us be reminded that our understanding of what the text says and means today begins in what the text said and meant for the original author and recipients. That is, the original meaning must guide our understanding today. Adding to the difficulty in our reading and understanding, the books of Thessalonians, and especially this chapter, have some of the characteristics of apocalyptic literature, suggesting that we should be thinking in terms of symbols and figures and asking ourselves about the meaning of the symbols.

This chapter deals with a specific question related to the coming of the Lord (the coming of the Day of the Lord). Some were teaching that the coming of the Lord had already occurred. Paul speaks to what is currently happening, what must happen before that day comes, and what will happen when that day comes. Some writers have identified the antichrist in this chapter, but Paul does not make that connection. He does not use the word "antichrist" to describe the opposing force. In fact, to speak of "the Antichrist" is to speak where the Bible does not speak. The Bible speaks of many antichrists rather than only one (1 John 2:18-19). There is no justification for inserting into the text ideas and concepts that are not divinely inspired. In this passage, the Bible never makes the identification of the lawless one as an antichrist. By the way, this commitment to describing biblical ideas or concepts in the same way the Bible describes them is why I do not use the phrase "second coming." It is not a phrase that is used in the Bible.

STUDY HELPS

2:1-4. This chapter expands Paul's teachings in 1 Thessalonians 4 and 5. Paul uses the word *parousia* to describe Jesus' coming or future presence, just as in the first letter. Not only does Paul use *parousia* to describe Christ's return, he describes the same event as "our gathering to him," in parallel to 1 Thess. 4:13-18. These verses (2:1-4) speak of one "coming," not two, and thus contradict traditional pre-tribulational, premillennial theory. "Concerning the coming of Jesus and our being gathered to him" combines the two ideas and suggests a continuation of the subject of 1 Thessalonians 4 and 5. The idea that other comings of Jesus could be in view is not supported by the context.

Paul urges that the Thessalonians not be easily moved from their previous understanding of the return of Christ (1 Thess. 5:1-2), and that they not be disturbed, whether by spirit (prophetic teaching), message, or letter claiming to be from Paul. The content of the false teaching was that the day of the Lord had already come. For other New Testament uses of the phrase "day of the Lord," see Acts 2:20 (quotation from Joel); 1 Cor. 5:5, 2 Cor. 1:14, and 2 Pet. 3:1, 10. The remainder of the New Testament uses of the phrase are in the Thessalonian correspondence: 1 Thess. 5:1, 2; and 2 Thess. 2:2. Our study of the phrase must begin with Old Testament usage, especially in the prophets. Two general options are possible: (1) a day of judgment or a day of blessing within history, and (2) the end of time at the end of history.

2:3. Do not be deceived. The "day" cannot come until the rebellion (apostasy) comes first, and the man of lawlessness (of sin) "is revealed," described as "the son of destruction" (having a destroying nature, one who brings destruction, the same phrase is used to describe Judas Iscariot in John 17:12). The phrase means "destined for destruction."

The idea of "revelation" is not to be confused with "appearing." That the identity of someone has been revealed is different than affirming that the person has appeared or is present.

Two events are mentioned: an apostasy and the revealing of the man of lawlessness (literally, the text reads, "unless should come the apostasy first and unless should be revealed the man of lawlessness"). To describe the apostasy here as "great" goes beyond what the text says. Apostasy is rebellion, literally "to stand away from." Apostasies are mentioned in 1 Timothy 4 and 2 Timothy 3. The man of lawlessness will be revealed (*apocalupsis*, the normal word for revelation). The idea of "revelation" is not to be confused with "appearing." To know the identity of someone is different than affirming that the person has appeared or is present. There is a variant in the Greek manuscripts concerning "lawlessness" or "sin." The reading of "lawlessness" is almost certain.

The use of "man" (*anthropos*) leads us to think of a specific individual. In v. 6, "he" will be revealed (the construction can be either personal or impersonal). In v. 7 we have the mystery of lawlessness already working, and in v. 8, the text says "will be revealed (parallel verb, as in v. 3) the lawless one (an impersonal construction)." The importance and interpretation of these grammatical factors are explained further in the comments on vv. 7-8.

The idea of revealing is used in the New Testament of Jesus' future coming. Connecting "revelation" and "coming" is possible, but it is also possible that "presence" (coming) could precede the "revelation." The construction used here does not necessarily mean that the "man of lawlessness" is not already present. (See my comments on v. 8, and the use of *parousia* in v. 9 to describe the lawless one.) The next verse (2:4) uses the present tense to describe already occurring activities of this lawless person. To summarize the significant message of v. 3: two conditions must precede the coming of "the day."

2:4. This verse begins with a description of the man of lawlessness. He is not Satan; his revelation is a work of Satan (v. 9). Based on the wording of the text, he is not identified as antichrist. Some have suggested he should be identified with the Jewish apocalyptic "worthless one" who was a false Messiah. He is man of lawlessness, son of destruction, (present tense) an opponent who places himself in an adversarial position, he opposes (sets himself against) and exalts himself above everything that is called god or considered to be an object of worship, so that he would seat himself in God's temple, thus setting himself forth as God. He will be judged and destroyed even though he appears to be divine.

"Temple of God" may be a literal reference to the temple in Jerusalem which was still standing at the date of the Thessalonian correspondence. The phrase may be a figurative reference to the church, although it is difficult to understand the figure. It could be understood as a reference to heaven. It may be a figurative reference to God's spiritual throne, simply indicating the desire of the lawless one to usurp the throne. The concept of usurping the throne is used in apocalyptic literature with reference to the Roman Empire (Rev. 12-13). The word "temple" was also used to describe pagan temples where deities were enthroned. The Greek temples had thrones; the other possibilities mentioned above did not. A figurative, apocalyptic interpretation does not depend on literal parallelism. The best interpretative option is figurative (we are dealing with apocalyptic literature): "so that he would take the place of God, claiming to be God."

Surely these verses had meaning to the Thessalonians. Parallel events from the same time period would include Caligula putting a statue of himself in the Jerusalem temple (about 10 years before this letter was written), the fall of Jerusalem in AD 70, and the reigns of terror and persecution unleashed by Nero and Domitian. What was the meaning for the Thessalonians? A lawless person (one embodying lawlessness) would be revealed before the Day of the Lord could come.

2:5-12. This section is one of the more difficult passages in the Bible. It will be helpful to keep in mind that the passage is similar to apocalyptic literature.

2:5-6. Paul had shared these teachings when he was with them. As previously noted, the Thessalonians had an orientation and knowledge that we do not have today. Notice the phrases, "do you not remember" (v. 5) and "you know" (v. 6).

At the present time ("now," referring to the time of Paul's writing) something is "holding back" (restraining). There is no direct object for the verb to indicate that the lawless man (lawless one, lawlessness) is the one being restrained. In the context of the verse, what is being restrained is the revealing. Literally, the verse reads, "And now you know the restraining thing unto (until) his revealing in his own time." Remember my comment earlier that revealing and appearing or presence are not necessarily simultaneous. As a result of Paul's previous teachings (v. 5), the Thessalonians understood what Paul was saying.

Holding back, *katecho*, appears in vv. 6 and 7. For other uses of the Greek word in the New Testament, see Lk. 4:42; 8:15; 14:9; Jn. 5:4; Acts 27:40; Rom. 1:18; 7:6; 1 Cor. 7:30; 11:2; 15:2; 2 Cor. 6:10; 1 Th. 5:21; Philm. 13; Heb. 3:6, 14; 10:23. In the context, restrain seems a good translation. The restraining is temporary, and the revelation will come "in his/its time" (in the future). The restraint focuses the fact that the revelation has not yet occurred, and that the revelation (of the lawless one) must occur before the coming of the day of the Lord.

A frequently asked question is, what is the restraining thing? We notice a grammatical change from neuter (vv. 6-7) to masculine (vv. 7-8). This likely indicates personification so that we are not seeking a specific individual. Traditional interpretations of the restraining power include the Roman Empire, a certain Roman emperor, the preaching of the gospel, or the Holy Spirit. The restraining power is a reality at the time of the writing of the letter. The restraining power is under God's control and is part of God's plan (vv. 6-7). At the right future time, the restraining thing will be removed (taken out of the midst) and the revelation will occur.

2:7. The mystery of lawless is already at work. Even before the revelation of the man of lawlessness (vv. 3 and 4), lawlessness is at work. Lawlessness is not exclusively the result of the revelation of a certain man (man of lawlessness). The one who is yet to be revealed in his [own] time will simply participate in and have the same nature as the lawlessness that already exists.

Mystery signifies something previously unknown but now revealed (or to be revealed in the future). NET translates this section: "the hidden power of lawlessness is already at work." Lawlessness is already present when Paul writes, but will be personified in the future in the one who is to be revealed or is to come.

The restraining one (power) will continue restraining until he/it is (*ginomai*) out of the middle, no longer in the way. The "one" who restrains (v. 7) contrasts with the impersonal use in v. 6 (the thing that restrains). The restraint is described both as a force and as personal.

2:8. Then (after the previous things have occurred) the lawless one will be revealed. Remember that Paul's point is that the day of the Lord cannot have already come, because there must first be rebellion (apostasy) and the revealing of the lawless one (lawless man, lawless force, lawlessness).

The lawless one (lawless man, lawlessness) has not yet been revealed because there is a restraining force or person (although lawlessness is already at work in possibly hidden ways). Eventually this restraining force will no longer be present, opening the way for the things described in v. 8.

Then the lawless one will be revealed, the one whom the Lord will destroy with the spirit of his mouth and annul with the appearance (*epiphania*) of his coming (*parousia*). The construction of the verse with appositive descriptive phrases does not require chronological connection. That is, the events of vv. 8-9 do not have to be understood as sequential. The first part of the verse is future event; the second part of the verse is descriptive: "this is the one whom the Lord will destroy...." Literally the text reads, "this is the one the Lord will take away with the breath of his mouth and render powerless by the appearance of his coming." Appearance is *epiphania*, coming is *parousia*. The last part of v. 8 can occur a long time after the first part of the verse since it is only descriptive, almost parenthetical. To resume v. 9 where v. 8a stopped would be normal with this kind of construction.

Considering that this is apocalyptic language, v. 8 ("with the breath of his mouth") may remind us of Revelation 19 where we read about power coming from the mouth. The power of spirit of the mouth could signify the gospel, or it could simply paint a vivid picture of death and destruction coming from the mouth of Jesus. The use of *parousia* seems to place the ultimate destruction at Jesus' return.

2:9. The construction, "of whom the coming is according to the working of Satan...." shows that "of whom" points back to the lawless one. Again, this highlights the nature of the descriptive phrase in v. 8.

A more literal translation of vv. 8 and 9 will demonstrate the exact construction: "then will be revealed the <u>lawless one</u>, (<u>which</u> the Lord will destroy by the spirit of his mouth and overthrow with the appearance of his coming,) <u>of whom</u> the coming is according to the working of Satan...."

In vv. 8 and 9, *parousia* is applied both to Jesus (v. 8) and to the lawless one (v. 9). Parousia is literally "being alongside," sometimes translated presence. Thinking about the future presence of one not now present, it is understood and translated as "coming."

The work of the lawless one is according to Satan's working (activity), capable of miracles and signs and false wonders. It will look as though the lawless one is doing great things, but they will in fact be false. Miracles can be counterfeited.

2:10. These are all unrighteous deceptions "to those who are perishing, of whom the love of the truth was not received unto their salvation." The text says those who are perishing are the ones deceived. Those deceived are those who did not accept the love of the truth, or refused to love the truth.

2:11. This working of deception or error is attributed to God. Because of this, that is, because of their failure to love the truth (v. 12), God sends a deceptive working (unrighteous influence) so they believe what is false. The plural refers to the same ones as v. 10. In this matter, God can be actively or passively involved and still be in control of the events of the world.

The timing or sequencing of vv. 7-11 is significant and must be noted. Consider this paraphrase that helps to clarify the message of this passage:

(7) Lawlessness is at work in the time of the Thessalonians, but the lawless one has not yet been revealed due to the presence of a restrainer; but when the restraining influence is no longer present, (8) the lawless one will be revealed. (This is one who the Lord will destroy and overthrow at his coming.) (9) The coming of the lawless one is by Satan's working and (10) evil deception against those who are perishing. Some perish because they did

not receive a love for the truth that would result in their salvation. (11) Therefore [in the coming of the lawless one] God sends on them a deluding influence so they believe falsehood. (12) The result will be that all who have not believed truth but have delighted in evil will be judged [condemned].

The verses say nothing about the timing of the events described, only that they are future. One may identify a more immediate anticipation of the revelation of the lawless one for the Thessalonians, but the text does not demand such immediacy. Perhaps the revelation of the lawless one and his presence as one who does Satan's works will lead to apostasy or rebellion. This explanation would suggest a first-last-last-first construction in v. 3. Before the day of the Lord, rebellion (apostasy) must come and the revelation of the lawless one must occur. The revelation of the lawless one will be like this, with the result that the rebellion (apostasy) will follow.

2:12. The condemnation comes from the deception, the lack of love for truth, the delusion, believing what is false, and enjoying evil. The result is that condemnation follows. All those who belong to the group described will be judged and condemned.

Whoever the man of lawlessness is, his influence and impact come through deceptions associated with Satan so that he is able to influence people away from truth ("without love for truth") so they will not be saved. The presence of an influence that deludes or deceives causes people to believe falsehoods. Because such people do not believe truth but delight in evil, they will be condemned. In seeking to apply these verses, the question arises whether Christians or unbelievers are being described. The application to unbelievers is not difficult to see. The context does not clearly apply this description to those who become Christians but are afterward influenced away from Christ. However, the connection of the rebellion and the revealing the man of lawlessness in v. 3, as explained in the comments on 2:11, could suggest such an application to first-century Christians.

Summary of Chapter 2:1-12

The Thessalonians can know that the day of the Lord has not yet come because the rebellion and lawlessness Paul had taught them about has not occurred.

It would seem that Paul had warned the Thessalonians about a specific individual or the presence of a lawless force, which would lead to rebellion or apostasy. For the modern reader, it is difficult to identify the specific individual or influence that existed in the first century. The abiding lesson is that lawlessness is always at work, sometimes stronger and sometimes weaker as a result of various restraining factors in our culture and world. Any time that restraints are removed, lawlessness increases.

The specific situation Paul mentions is still future in his day. When it occurs, it will demonstrate the power of lawlessness as a force, or the power of some specific individual or influence toward lawlessness. Nonetheless, the assurance remains that all such lawlessness will be destroyed and overthrown at Jesus' coming. (In the context, the day of the Lord has not come; it is clear that Jesus has not returned because the anticipated rebellion and the revelation of the lawless one have not occurred, even as lawlessness continues to exist.) The lawless one will be revealed; the lawless one will be destroyed at Jesus' coming (which has not yet occurred).

2:13-17. Paul again mentions constant prayer (always), thanking God for the salvation of the Thessalonians who are beloved by God. Notice the references—God, Lord, Spirit. The Thessalonian church is the first fruits of the gospel, through sanctification by the Spirit and their belief (faith) in the truth. This description highlights the two-fold dimension of salvation—God's work and human response. God's work among the Thessalonians is contrasted with the description of 2:11-12, those who do not believe because they do not love the truth. The work of God described in v. 13 is consistent with the calling of God and results in glory for the believers (cf. 2 Thess. 1:11-12). God calls human beings to him through the truth of the gospel.

2:15-17. "Brothers" introduces the conclusion of this chapter. Christians must stand firm (persevere) and hold the traditions (that which has been passed down) of Paul's teachings.

The chapter closes with a prayer. Paul's prayer is that Jesus Christ, and God the Father who loved us and gave us eternal comfort and good hope, will comfort (encourage) the hearts of the Thessalonians and establish them in every good work and word. The comfort and hope received from Christ and the Father will encourage and establish the Thessalonians.

2 Thessalonians 3

[Note: especially for those who are not familiar with the five step Bible study process, it is suggested that the introductory materials concerning paragraphing be read before beginning your own preparatory reading and analysis.]

CONTENT

The paragraphing and outline included in the Content section of each chapter are only intended as suggestions or guides. The student is encouraged to identify the paragraphs and subparagraphs as part of his or her own study using a personal study Bible. The division of this chapter into paragraphs is fairly standard in modern translations.

Outline of the Chapter

3:1-5	An appeal: "pray for us, even as we pray for your perseverance"
3:6-15	Warning against idleness and disunity
3:16-18	Concluding words

Observations about the Contents of the Chapter

The construction of the book of 2 Thessalonians is interesting. Virtually all of the first chapter serves as an introduction to the letter. The third chapter serves as the closing, with the principal theme explained and expounded in the second chapter. In this closing chapter, Paul requests prayers, affirms God's faithfulness, warns against problems that had arisen due to the misunderstandings about Jesus' coming, and closes the letter in typical fashion.

Overview: Summary of the Message

"In conclusion, pray for the message to keep on spreading as it did when it came to you. Pray that we can escape evil. God is faithful. We are confident; we believe he will provide strength and protection in the love and endurance of Christ.

"A final matter—you have to stay away from undisciplined brothers who teach things contrary to the message you have received from us. When we were among you, we gave you an example of what it means to work hard. Those who refuse to work should not eat! When people quit working they start meddling. Live right, work hard, keep on, and separate yourselves from anyone who won't live by these basic teachings. Maybe they will wake up and change. These wayward brothers are not enemies—be kind in your dealings with them.

"May God give us peace always through his presence. I am giving you my customary greetings in my own handwriting. Grace!"

STUDY HELPS
The two principal sections of the chapter (1) reflect Paul's desire to continue preaching the gospel with God's blessing and (2) give a warning about some actions that stem from misunderstandings about Jesus' coming.

3:1-5. "Finally" is literally "for the rest." We might say "as to the rest." This phrase is transitional; in this case, it marks the beginning of the conclusion. Paul's first request is this: pray for us that the gospel will spread and be glorified (cf. 2 Thess. 1:11-12). A second request is for protection and rescue from evil men. Not all are willing to receive the truth of the gospel (2 Thess. 2:11-12). Our faithful God will strengthen you and protect you from evil (either neuter or masculine), possibly referring to the evil one (Satan), but in the context referring to protection from all kinds of evil, including the false teachers and those who do evil because they reject the truth.

Paul is confident in the Lord that the Thessalonians are doing and will keep on doing the things commanded (teachings, traditions, literally "the things passed down"). He prays for them, that the Lord will guide them into greater love and steadfastness, even as he asks them to pray for him.

3:6-15. Paul now turns to the second topic of this chapter: warnings concerning the actions of some of the brothers at Thessalonica. Paul commands that they keep away from idle (undisciplined, lazy, not working) brothers who do not keep the teachings (traditions) received from Paul. Idle is "disorderly conduct." The context suggests that some believers, in anticipation of the immediate return of Jesus, had ceased working. They expected to be supported by the other Christians. Different understandings often lead to disagreements and an uncooperative, disorderly spirit. Paul urges all to honor the teaching he has passed on to them (what they had received).

In vv. 7-9, Paul reminds them of his example when he was among them—how he worked and did not depend on others, how he paid what was due when he received something from others, and how he kept on working night and day in the midst of much labor and hardship. He had the right to do otherwise, but he did not use that right. And even during his presence with them he gave the same order, "that those who would not work should not eat." This was apparently not a new problem in Thessalonica.

3:11-12. This text uses a word play on the Greek word "work." The ESV captures the thought like this: "We hear that some among you walk in idleness, not busy at work, but busybodies." Building on the concept of "busy at work" one could translate: "We hear that some are not busy working, but are busybodies, interfering with everyone else's busy-ness." Paul's response was to command and exhort in the Lord that everyone should work quietly and earn their own living. "Quiet" is parallel in meaning to 1 Thess. 4:11 where the same Greek word is used.

3:13-15. "Do not grow weary of doing good" is similar to Gal. 6:9. Other people watch how we Christians live. If someone in the church will not obey the command (v. 12), that person should be identified (noted, tagged, marked) and avoided (as in v. 6), so he will be ashamed. This appears to be a complete disfellowship as in 1 Cor. 5. The same word is used in both passages (occurring only here and in 1 Cor. 5). The goal of church discipline is to correct and restore.

3:16-18. In verse 16 is a closing prayer. As Paul opened and closed the first letter with salutations that mentioned peace, so also here in the second letter: "the God of peace." The closing verses of the two Thessalonian letters are similar. May the God of peace grant you peace. In v. 17, Paul affirms with his own hand his authorship. Paul dictated his letters to an amanuensis (scribe, secretary), but included a final section written with his own hand. In v. 18, Paul mentions grace, again reflecting the beginning of the letter. The plural (all of you) indicates that the letter was intended for the entire church.

Made in the USA
Middletown, DE
11 November 2022

14677440R00076